LOCKLEAZE SCHOOLS

The Wheatsheaf

LOCKLEAZE SECONDARY SCHOOL

No. 3

OCTOBER 1957

The front cover of the October 1957 edition of the school magazine, *The Wheatsheaf.* The first issue, which was published in 1955 (the year after the school opened), had much of the spirit of the new pioneer school about it, proud of what had been achieved in its first year. The school badge, representing a wheatsheaf, is featured on the cover. A wheatsheaf was chosen as the school emblem because when the first head took over his far-from-finished school in 1954 the land around was still being cultivated and wheat sheaves piled in stooks – pyramids of drying grain – were a common sight in the surrounding fields. The Latin school motto was *Fidelis ad Finem* (Faithful to the End).

BRITAIN IN OLD PHOTOGRAPHS

LOCKLEAZE SCHOOLS

IAN HADDRELL

The
History
Press

Cover picture: Taken in 1955, the year after Lockleaze Secondary School opened, this class photograph of pupils who started in September 1955, includes the school's first headmaster, Mr H.S. Whaley. Horace Stanley Whaley (1913–1998) is seated on the first row and is easily identified by his spectacles and the characteristic flower in his buttonhole. He left Lockleaze to join Monk's Park School, as its first headmaster when it opened in 1957, being succeeded at Lockleaze by Dr W.N. Littlejohns. From left to right, back row: Paul Brookman, Michael Poole, Jeffrey Harrap, Michael Jackson, Jeffrey Russell, David Richardson, Colin Hanks, Anthony Read, Alan Elvins. Third row: Tony Pople, Lynda Hedgeland, Sonja Forse, Cynthia Hole, Valerie Ratcliffe, Pearl Noble, Jennifer Archer, Janet Shorland, Jacqueline Hocking. Second row: Wendy Morgan, Patricia Tarr, Mr K.A. Edwards – deputy headmaster, Mr R.C. Clouter, Mr H.S. Whaley, Mr A. Robertson, Angela Slater. Front row: Jeffrey Slowley, Norman Bryant, Desmond Tippins, James Honey, Robert Logan. Other class members included: David Andrews, Yvonne Derrick, Christine Dugdale, John Hill, Philip Lanceley, Carol Northam, Christopher Parrott.

First published 2008

The History Press Ltd.
The Mill, Brimscombe Port
Stroud, Gloucestershire, GL5 2QG
www.thehistorypress.co.uk

© Ian Haddrell, 2008

The right of Ian Haddrell to be identified as the Author
of this work has been asserted in accordance with the
Copyrights, Designs and Patents Act 1988.

British Library Cataloguing in Publication Data.
A catalogue record for this book is available from the British Library.

ISBN 978 0 7524 4754 4

Printed in Great Britain

CONTENTS

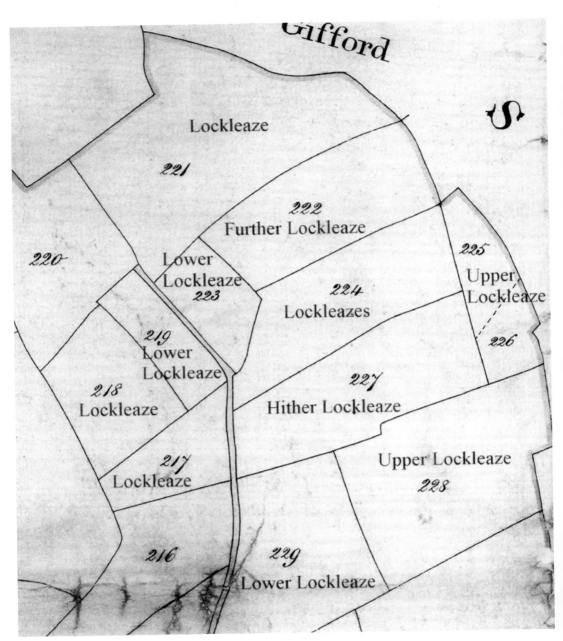

Detail of the 1843 Horfield Tithe Map, showing fields in the north-eastern corner of the parish that adjoins the parishes of Stapleton and Stoke Gifford. The ancient field names in this area include; Lockleaze, Lock Leaze, Lockleazes, Further Lockleaze, Hither Lockleaze, Lower Lockleaze and Upper Lockleaze. Lockleaze Secondary Modern School was built in field No. 221, named Lockleaze. The un-named track ending at field No. 220 is Lockleaze Lane, which ran from Horfield Court Farm via Berry Lane Farm to the variously named Lockleaze fields.

INTRODUCTION

LOCKLEAZE

At the beginning of the nineteenth century the parish of Horfield contained a few farms and cottages, and had a population of just 119 in 1801. Many of these lived near the common where any who had commoner's rights could graze one horse, two cows or three yearlings. The farms, mostly pastureland, varied considerably in size from 260 acres down to 4 acres. Two farms faced each other at the northern end of the common. Demolished in 1905, Horfield Court Farmhouse, on the east side, was the oldest building in Horfield with some fine oak-panelled rooms. It is remembered in the name Court Road. Manor Farm faced it from the western side.

The 1843 Tithe Map of Horfield shows an un-named track which is identified on the 1881 Ordnance Survey Map as Lockleaze Lane. At the far end of Lockleaze Lane was Lockleaze Farm, an isolated farmhouse located on the site now occupied by the terrace of houses along the north-east side of Thornycroft Close and houses on the west side of Bonnington Walk. Lockleaze Farm, built between 1843 and 1851, is recorded by name in each of the decennial census enumerations from 1851 to 1901, and in 1851 Edward Robertson, a farm bailiff from Malmesbury, occupied the farm, comprising 50 acres. In 1901 the farm was inhabited by fifty-seven-year-old farmer James Saunders and his family, by which time the population of Horfield parish, in which Lockleaze Farm resided, had increased to 6,712 inhabitants.

The origin of the name Lockleaze for the moment remains uncertain. The suffix Leaze, from the Old English (OE) *læs* is a common field name, denoting open communal pasture or meadow; *loc*, another OE word, means fold (in the land). A possible interpretation therefore is 'fold in a meadow or pasture'.

POST-WAR DEVELOPMENT

Lockleaze is an area in the northern suburbs of Bristol, three miles north of the city centre. It is a long narrow residential area built on the western flank of Pur Down on a north-south axis, separated from Horfield by a main railway line. The suburb was developed immediately after the Second World War to assist the housing shortage. The Lockleaze estate's layout is in part influenced by the ideas of the garden suburb movement, resulting in the relatively low density of development and generous garden areas. The overall layout of the estate is relatively formal and generally spacious with most homes being set back from the street with substantial front and rear gardens. There are also a large number of formal open spaces spread throughout the estate and some backland areas that have previously been developed for allotments and other uses.

Bristol's council-house building – which really got into its stride in the 1920s – marked a complete break from the style and layout of the old, privately built neighbourhoods like Bedminster and Easton. These municipally built low-density, cottage-type houses, built in pairs or short rows with sizeable gardens, contrasted strongly with the old Victorian terraces, and were generally of better quality than anything that could be offered to families in the private rented sector and, indeed, were often superior to affordable owner-occupied housing. In the immediate post-war period, when the major objective of housing policy was to increase supply, the construction of houses by the local authority took off dramatically. There was now a more comprehensive approach to the planning of these estates, with Bristol Corporation trying to make provision for more than just family housing. At this time a serious shortage of building land within the city boundaries led the council to make an application to the Boundary Commission to double the size of the city.

Lockleaze was purchased before the start of the Second World War but development did not commence until 1946, after the war had ended. The original material palette used in Lockleaze comprised a simple set of complimentary materials. These generally included a mixture of rendered concrete precast sections and red/brown concrete tiles, or brown brickwork and brown concrete roof tiles. Joyce Storey, who lived at No. 113 Landseer Avenue, describes the new estate in her book *The House in South Road*:

… in the spring sunshine, the avenue was a delight with the misty-pink blossom of the newly planted Japanese cherry trees. The pastel pinks, greens and greys of the painted houses blended with the foliage and clustered blossom of these trees. Every so often along the avenue there were cul-de-sacs, in front of which were large grassland play areas, which had been planted by the Council with young saplings that looked as though they had been retained from the original meadow.

The Conventional District of Lockleaze was formed from the parishes of Stapleton, Horfield and St Gregory, Horfield in 1948 by Order in Council, becoming the parish of St Mary Magdalene with St Francis, Lockleaze on 1 March 1962. Conventional District is the name given to a new church district which is on probation for a few years before being made a parish.

STREET NOMENCLATURE

When Lockleaze was completed Bristol Housing Department decided for the first time to enter the artistic field and to name the various roads after eminent British artists, some familiar, others not so familiar. With the adjoining Horfield estate following the literary trend, it was perhaps apt that another of the arts should be selected for Lockleaze. H.C.W. Harris, a former housing manager with Bristol City Council, compiled a booklet in 1969 entitled 'Housing Nomenclature in Bristol', being the origin of road and flat names used in Municipal Housing in Bristol between 1919 and 1967, which includes details of the origins of Lockleaze road names.

Name	Origin
Blake Road	William Blake (1757-1827). Painter, engraver, poet and mystic. Perhaps best remembered for *Jerualem* and 'Tyger! Tyger! burning bright' from *The Tyger*.
Bonnington Walk	Richard Parkes Bonington (1801-1827). An English Romantic landscape painter, he spent most of his time in France but died on a visit to England. The correct spelling is with one 'n'.
Brangwyn Grove	Sir Frank Brangwyn (1867-1956). Born in Bruges of Welsh parents. Noted for mural decorations, but was also an artist of repute.
Branwhite Close	Charles Branwhite (1817-1880). Bristol-born landscape artist whose father, Nathan, was a well-known miniature artist.
Constable Road	John Constable (1776-1837). The most celebrated of all British landscape painters. His pictures 'The Hay Wain' and 'Dedham Mill' are familiar to most people.
Copley Gardens	John Singleton Copley (1737-1815). Portrait painter in oil and crayons. Born Boston, Massachusetts but settled in London in 1776.
Cotman Walk	John Sell Cotman (1782-1842). Landscape painter, chiefly in watercolours. Of the Norwich School.
Crome Road	John Crome (1768-1821). Landscape painter. Born in humble circumstances, he founded the Norwich School of painting.
Danby House	Francis Danby (1793-1861). Painter of ideal and poetic landscapes. Two of his sons, James Francis and Thomas, were also artists.
Downman Road	John Downman (1750-1824). Portrait and subject painter. His exquisite pencil portrait drawings, slightly tinted in colour, usually from the reverse, are well known.
Eastlake Close	Sir Charles Lock Eastlake (1793-1865). Painter, art collector and writer, he was the first pupil of Benjamin Haydon. President of the Royal Academy 1850-1865 and first director of the National Gallery.
Flaxman Close	John Flaxman (1755-1826). Sculptor and draughtsman. Possibly the most eminent of British sculptors.
Gainsborough Square	Thomas Gainsborough (1727-1788). Mainly a portrait painter and supreme in his own field. 'The Blue Boy' is perhaps his most famous painting.
Gilray Close	James Gilray or Gillray (1757-1813). Caricaturist and printmaker famous for his etched political and social satires.
Haydon Gardens	Benjamin Robert Haydon (1786-1846). Historical painter and writer. Well known as a lecturer on painting and design.
Herkomer Close	Sir Hubert von Herkomer (1849-1914). Portrait and subject painter. Born in Bavaria, he was brought to England in 1857 and subsequently naturalised.

Highmore Gardens	Joseph Highmore (1692-1780). Portrait and subject painter. Among his best works are biblical 'Histories'.
Hogarth Walk	William Hogarth (1697-1764). Painter, engraver and caricaturist. Noted for his series of studies of low life.
Landseer Avenue	Sir Edwin Henry Landseer (1802-1873). Animal painter who also excelled in painting portraits of children. Landseer sculptured the lions for the Nelson Monument in Trafalgar Square.
Linnell Close	John Linnell (1792-1882). Portrait and landscape painter. Friend of William Blake.
Morris Road	William Morris (1834-1896). Perhaps better known as a poet and writer and for his private printing activities than as an artist.
Mulready Close	William Mulready (1786-1863). Painter and book illustrator, best known for his romanticising depictions of rural scenes. Designed the first penny postage envelope issued by Rowland Hill in 1840.
Nash Drive	Paul Nash (1889-1946). Watercolourist of great individuality. An official war artist during both world wars.
Orpen Gardens	Sir William Newnham Montague Orpen (1878-1931). Irish-born portrait painter. He was made an official war painter of the First World War in 1917.
Rackham Close	Arthur Rackham (1867-1939). A prolific book illustrator whose major works include *Alice's Adventures in Wonderland* and *Rip van Winkle*.
Romney Avenue	George Romney (1734-1802). A noted portrait painter, but his 'The Death of General Wolfe' is well known.
Rowlandson Gardens	Thomas Rowlandson (1756-1827). Artist and caricaturist. With Gilray and Hogarth probably the most famous British caricaturist.
Stanfield Close	Clarkson Stanfield (1793-1867). Marine and landscape painter. Regarded by Ruskin as 'the leader of the English realists'.
Stothard Close	Thomas Stothard (1755-1834). Painter, engraver and book illustrator. Friend of William Blake.
Thornycroft Close	Sir William Hamo Thornycroft (1850-1925). Sculptor of numerous public monuments throughout Britain and the Empire.
Turner Gardens	Joseph Mallord William Turner (1775-1851). Landscape painter in Romantic style. A prolific artist, his most famous work is 'The Fighting Temeraire'.

THE SCHOOLS

The system of national school education envisaged by the Butler Education Act of 1944, guaranteeing secondary education for all, was established in the city of Bristol with nursery, primary, secondary and further education all provided by Bristol Education Committee. One of the most obvious features of post-war education in Bristol was the establishment of secondary schools, beginning in Hengrove and Lockleaze in 1954.

Lockleaze Secondary Modern School, Hogarth Walk, by the City Architect's Department (project architect D.W. Salter, main contractor Holland & Hannen and Cubitts, Ltd) was built in 1951-1954, and extended in 1958-1959 under A.H. Clarke. The prototype of Bristol's early movement towards system building in schools, long-span prestressed reinforced concrete beams were used to offset the cost and uncertain availability of steel at that time. The structure is a precast frame with prestressed floors and brick panel walling. Bristol and Somerset were two of the leaders in the development of 'Method Building', but this building anticipated this by several years in its modular design and treatment. T.H.B. Burrough, a renowned local architect who designed St Mary's in Gainsborough Square, commented in 1970 that, 'This school is ahead of its time'. The school opened in September 1954 and closed in 2004.

Lockleaze Junior and Infants Schools, Romney Avenue, by Richard Sheppard & Geoffrey Robson, were built in 1948-1950. The prototype of Bristol Aeroplane Co.'s (BAC's) Mark I prefabricated school-building system, pressed aluminium was used throughout, intended to take up the slack in their former aircraft factories once the need for prefabricated housing was filled by 1948. The junior school completed in 1949 (the infant and nursery schools to the north, a year later) consisted of brick-built halls and entrance, two long classroom blocks in parallel running north, with continuous glazing to the front and canted fins expressing the classroom divisions. Most fixtures and furnishings were of pressed aluminium.

The infant school was altered internally by Kendall Kingscott, in 2005-2006, and opened in September 2006, following the amalgamation of Romney Avenue Infants and Junior Schools. Lockleaze Primary School is situated in a newly refurbished spacious modern building with extensive grounds and play areas. The junior school was demolished after closure in August 2006.

ACKNOWLEDGEMENTS

I would like to thank the following for supplying photographs and information for this book: Terry Annette, Stuart Armsby, Lesley Beacham (née Freestone), Steven Bevan, Bishopston, Horfield and Ashley Down Local History Society, Bristol Archaeological Research Group, Bristol Central Library, *Bristol Evening Post*, *Bristol Evening World*, Bristol Record Office, Alan Brown, Andy Buchan, *Building*, T.H.B. Burrough, Douglas H. Byles, Carol Channon (née Northam), Heather Cunningham (née Plummer), Hazel Day (née Jarrett), Michael Day, Jenny Dunford, Derek Fisher, Andy Foyle, Wendy Gage (née Harding), Jean Gleed (née Gadsby), Gloucestershire Record Office, Neil Greatorex, Mike Gwilliam, Diane Haddrell (née Stone), Doreen Hazell, Michael A. Houlden, Angela Knight (née Cooper), Mrs Joy Langley, Carole Lavis, Lockleaze Primary School, Lockleaze Secondary School, John Lyes, Andrew and Liz Malpas, Greg Malpas, Ernest Marvin, Carole Meyer (née Brewer), Gillian McKenzie (née Smalldridge), Valerie Nash (née Cooper), Josephine Naylor (née Conlin), Christine Palmer (née Badman), Andy Parker, Brenda Parrott (née Cooper), Joyce Plummer, Reg Porter, Teresa Purkis, P.D. Rendall, Michael Richardson, Nicholas Roberts, Lindra Rowles (née Shore), Andrew Saint, Keith Smith, Martin Smyth, Valerie Stone (née Nash), Marion Strange (née Hawker), *The Surveyor and Municipal and County Engineer*, John Trenchard, Michael Wall, John Watson, Michael Watson, Wendy Williams (née Annette), Rose White (née Watts), Roland Williams and the Reece Winstone Collection.

A special thank you to Neil Bartle, whose encyclopaedic knowledge of Lockleaze Secondary School has been invaluable in providing countless facts, dates of events and identification of ex-members of staff.

My grateful thanks to my wife, Diane, for her support, tolerance, and contribution in making this book a success.

Every effort has been made to identify copyright holders of illustrations from published materials, but I apologise to anyone overlooked in my search, or to photograph owners, should their names be omitted from the above list.

1

DEVELOPMENT OF LOCKLEAZE

Looking north at a train arriving at Ashley Hill Station from Patchway, *c.*1910. The station and line, known as the Bristol to South Wales Union Railway, opened in 1863. Note the rural setting – the fields on the right of the picture will become part of Lockleaze suburb in forty years time, with Downman Road and Morris Road occupying the land at the top of the slope. Muller Road has not been constructed yet.

'Off For Their Annual Outing.' A procession of girls from Müllers Orphanage, in their distinctive uniforms, winds its way up to Purdown on their annual outing. Within walking distance from the orphanage, it was a most popular event. The orphanage, built in 1862, is the large building on the skyline. The card was posted in 1921.

Looking towards Purdown, this photograph was taken in 1897 from nearly opposite the Wellington Inn on Horfield Common. At their meeting on 12 July 1938, Bristol City Councillors accepted the Housing Committee's proposal to buy from Mrs R.G. Burden, an area of just over 112 acres between Purdown and the railway line for housing purposes. Some members expressed reservations because they thought that the price of £183 per acre was too high.

Two Edwardian ladies take a walk to the fields of Purdown in 1904 along a track, leading to Sir John's Lane, which is now covered by Shaldon Road and the commencement of Romney Avenue. Muller Road, built in the 1930s, now occupies the low ground between the foot of the hill and the railway embankment. Ashley Hill Station and Müllers Orphanage are in the distance. A young boy flies his kite on the right of the picture.

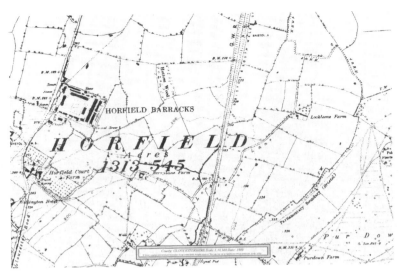

Practically the whole of Horfield parish, shown on this 1889 Ordnance Survey map, is common land, pasture or arable fields. The only indications of population are four farmhouses, the Wellington Hotel and Horfield Barracks. The foundation stone was laid in 1845 and the finished barracks handed over to the Board of Ordnance in 1847. The Duke of Wellington, who visited the barracks on a number of occasions, was a popular hero, and the local inn called the Ship was renamed the Wellington Hotel in his honour. The original inn was later rebuilt. The fields to the east of the railway line to Purdown became the Lockleaze estate in the 1940s.

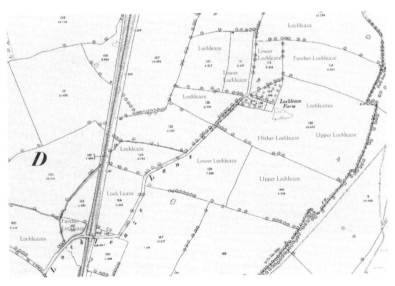

Lockleaze Farm, Lockleaze Lane and the main railway line are identifiable features on the 1881 Ordnance Survey map of part of Horfield parish. Lockleaze School was built 1951-1954 on the 12-acre field numbered 113, named 'Lockleaze', to the north of the farm. The relevant Lockleaze field names from the 1843 Tithe Apportionment have been added.

Early stages of construction of Lockleaze estate are evident from the road building taking place in this aerial photograph from 1946. Brangwyn Grove, Constable Road, Cotman Walk, Landseer Avenue, and Romney Avenue are in progress with, to the right of the line of trees, the outline of Gainsborough Square. Lockleaze Farm is in the bottom right of the picture.

Although of poor quality, this detail from the above photograph is the only known image of Lockleaze Farm. Awaiting demolition in 1946, the farm (built between 1843 and 1851) was located at the top of Lockleaze Lane, which is clearly visible running from the embryonic Constable Road to the farm buildings. The partially constructed road is Landseer Avenue, whilst the outline of Bonnington Walk heads towards the farm. The first known occupant, recorded in the 1851 census, was Edward Robertson, a farm bailiff. James Saunders, from Pensford, farmed the 55-acre farm from around 1880 until the 1920s. He and his family were probably the last inhabitants of the property.

Development of the estate is well under way in this aerial photograph taken in 1947. About a dozen roads have been finished with houses in various stages of construction. As yet, there are no shops, pubs or schools – the building contractor is using the site of the future secondary school as a storage yard. Lockleaze Farm, now demolished, stood on the land between the terraced houses in Thornycroft Close and Nos 86 and 88 Bonnington Walk.

Work has begun creating one of the first roads, Romney Avenue, on the new Lockleaze estate, in this 1946 photograph. Road construction was in sections and here concrete is being poured from the hopper suspended from the mobile crane. Pur Down Farm, later the site of Fairacre Close, can be seen on the skyline, its rural tranquillity about to become a thing of the past.

Five years later in 1951 and Romney Avenue is now alive with pedestrians and a variety of vehicles: cars, a bicycle, motorbike and sidecar, lorry, and a double-decker bus in the distance. Brangwyn Grove is the road on the left with Orpen Gardens opposite. The houses are complete and the new residents have moved into their homes.

2

LOCKLEAZE SECONDARY SCHOOL

On Friday 26 October 1956, for the fourth time since the Second World War, Bristol was honoured by a visit from the minister of education to open a group of new schools. On this occasion the Rt Hon. Sir David Eccles, the then minister, attended the official opening of twenty-one new primary and secondary schools at the Council House in College Green. Lockleaze Secondary School was one of the twenty-one local schools providing 8,810 places to be declared open that evening. The description of the school, below, is taken from the official programme published by Bristol Education Committee:

> The Building was originally designed as one of a pair of three-form entry schools to serve mainly the Lockleaze housing estate. Opened in September 1954, it was intended as the ultimate boys' school, to be shared initially by girls until their school was built later. It has now been decided that the school is to retain its mixed organisation, with an enlargement to six-form entry as soon as a place can be found for the extensions in a building programme. The school has a bilateral organisation at present and admissions are controlled by a boundary except for one form of selected children each year.

The school was on the drawing board in 1951-52, at a time when the early moves were developing towards the compactness which has now become such a basic part of school design. From the entrance hall, approached from Hogarth Walk, rises one of the two main staircases with the assembly hall and stage to the left and the gymnasium to the right. To the north-east extends the three-storey teaching block with views across playing fields and open country. The staff accommodation is planned in the three-storey block above the main entrance. A separate single-storey block, approached by means of a covered walkway, contains two workshops, two housecraft rooms, and the biology laboratory. The specially designed reinforced-concrete system, with long span prestressed beams now being used in a number of Bristol secondary schools, was first introduced at Lockleaze to offset the shortage of skilled site labour and the uncertain availability and high cost of structural steel.

The site of 13½ acres, which was enlarged at a later date, straddled the city boundary, and the playing fields merged into the surrounding farmlands and wooded countryside. The views, particularly from the classroom block, would have been most pleasing, particularly with the grounds maturing rapidly.

Lockleaze Secondary School showing the main entrance, assembly hall to the left and gymnasium to the right. The headmasters' and headmistresses' offices are the rooms immediately above the entrance. The building appears to be complete, but there is still some landscaping work to be done in this 1954 photograph.

Lockleaze was built as a secondary modern school, a type of secondary school that existed in most of the United Kingdom from 1944 until the early 1970s under the tripartite system, known colloquially as the grammar-school system. The system, prevalent under the Conservative governments of the 1950s and 1960s, divided secondary schools into three categories: grammar schools, technical schools and modern schools. After 1965, under a Labour government, it fell into disfavour and was formally abolished in 1976, giving way to the current comprehensive school system.

The landscaping of the school grounds is complete and the new school awaits its first pupils. On Monday 13 September 1954 the initial intake numbering 230 were admitted to 'Lockleaze County Secondary'. Duncan John Campbell of Brangwyn Grove was the first pupil entered in the new schools Admissions Register. The school comprised five first-year classes, one second-year class and one third-year class for the first term.

Looking from the main entrance foyer towards the single-storey block containing the workshops, housecraft rooms, and the biology laboratory. The covered walkway between the blocks was enclosed when additional classrooms were added between 1958 and 1959, becoming known as 'Rainbow Alley'. The 1959 issue of *The Wheatsheaf* is full of references to pneumatic drills, concrete mixers and mud, showing that Lockleaze was growing physically as well as intellectually.

The three-storey teaching block is now occupied and the playground put to good use by the first intake of pupils. This initial intake came from thirty different Bristol primary schools as well as St Winefride's, Southampton. The single-storey block on the right is the music room located at the rear of the stage in the main assembly hall.

The main entrance to the school, now named the Hogarth Building, following development of the site in the 1980s. The main assembly hall is the brick-faced building behind the school sign. The Channel 4 sitcom *Teachers*, broadcast between March 2001 and December 2004, was based at Lockleaze School. The first three series were set in the fictional Summerdown Comprehensive which merges with another school in the fourth series to form Watkins School. In 2004, eighteen weeks of a twenty-six week production schedule was spent filming the series in and around Lockleaze.

Christine Roberts is the girl walking towards the camera in this mid-1960s picture of the three-storey teaching block and playground. The boys always seemed to dominate this playground with their games of football and cricket. It was this part of the school that was used during the filming of the Channel 4 series *Teachers*.

Patricia Phillips, who started at the school in 1962, poses in her summer uniform in front of the tennis courts and science laboratory in 1968. The art rooms were situated on the first floor of this building.

Work has commenced on the new swimming pool being constructed on part of the school playing field, in this picture taken in 1968 from the needlework room. Funds for the construction of the pool were raised by energetic activities of parents, friends and pupils. One such fundraising event was 'Brown's Brew – A Mad Musical Miscellany' presented by the staff of the school. Saturday evening social events, whist drives and a huge fete held on the school field also helped to raise money for the project. Wally Lloyd, a Lockleaze resident and one-time chairman of the school governors, was a particularly active fundraiser. His daughter, Margaret, attended the school between 1956 and 1961, returning as Mrs Jones to teach mathematics.

Nearing completion: the exterior of the pool taken from the staff common room, 1968. The structure, a convex Perspex cover, stood on an 18in-high (0.45m) block base.

Inside the completed swimming pool building. There were no changing rooms in the new structure so pupils had to change in their respective sports changing rooms and then, in only swimming costume and blazer, walk to and from the pool. Not a pleasant experience in winter!

The school prospectus of the early 1960s describes Lockleaze School thus:

Lockleaze School is a comprehensive school for 1,100 boys and girls, maintained by the Bristol Education Committee. It is housed in new buildings opened in 1954 and provides secondary education of the very widest range and scope. Admission to the school is either by selection in what is usually known as the 'eleven plus', or by residence within the boundary laid down by the Education Committee. Other pupils are sometimes admitted. In their first year boys and girls are in Lower House. The premises are very attractive. There are five science laboratories, five housecraft rooms, four workshops and a drawing office: two art rooms, two geography rooms and music rooms: two gymnasia, two libraries and a fine stage for drama. There is every facility for advanced work in the sciences, the humanities, the arts and the crafts.

3

SCHOOL LIFE

THE SCHOOL CODE

Good work	High standards of work are always required. Homework is required because it teaches you to work on your own.
Good manners	You must always be polite and well-behaved Boys are to raise the cap to ALL adults they know. Pupils stand as the staff leave and enter rooms. Try always to speak clearly and well
Your property	Mark it - all of it. Keep money and valuables with you Caps to be kept in blazer pockets or satchels. Respect the property of others.
Your Prefects	Prefects share my authority and are responsible to me for what they do. They must therefore be obeyed. (You may be elected one day.)
Your clothes	Members of the School wear a distinctive uniform. For your parents' sake care for it and keep it clean. No jewellery nor non-school badges to be worn. (Any pupil not well-groomed brings shame on himself, his family and his School.)

The School	DO NOT	run in School. come in before 8.50. remain after 4 unless supervised. linger in cloakrooms etc.
	Dinner-hour	No movement about the building. Keep outside unless supervised.
	Litter	Don't drop any. Do clear up what others may leave.
	Corridors	Move on the left.
	Wet days	You may come straight into the form-room before school, and during the break and dinner hour, unless you are told otherwise.

W. N. Littlejohns

The school code was printed on the back cover of exercise books during the 1950s and early 1960s. This example from the time of Dr Littlejohns' headship includes the school rule – remarkable in this day and age – that 'Boys are to raise the cap to ALL adults they know'. The school's name and emblem were printed on the front cover. In 1969 standard Bristol Education Committee exercise books were introduced replacing the distinctive Lockleaze schoolbook; a circular map entitled 'Fifty Miles Around Bristol' adorned the reverse.

The brass section of the school orchestra, conducted by Mr Eric Brown, playing during the annual prize-giving on Thursday 22 October 1959. It was the first time that it had been possible to hold a full-scale upper school prize-giving, as for the previous year the staff and pupils had never been free from the noise and dirt of building operations. Reviewing the past year the headmaster Dr W.N. Littlejohns, said the school had been 'an educational octopus' in that classes were scattered around Bristol, giving rise to the school's private bus service. Owing to transport problems the guest of honour, Alderman St John Reade, chairman of Bristol Education Committee, was a quarter of an hour late in arriving, but the school orchestra struck up to fill the time.

The school library was located on the ground floor. The fashions and hairstyles of the pupils, presumably sixth-formers, place this photograph very much in the 1960s! Amongst the reading material on display are *The Times* newspaper, *Scala*, and *Stern*, a weekly German news magazine.

A biology lesson in the science laboratory, probably Mr Crowe's class 4.1 during school year 1969–70. From left to right: Diane Stone, Josephine Conlin, Linda Darby, Jennifer Hole, Wendy Annette. An animal skull with antlers never did catch on as a fashion accessory!

Written on the blackboard are the instructions and measurements ('Gauge and plane to thickness and width') for the boys to follow in their woodwork lesson in the 1960s. Woodwork, metalwork and technical drawing lessons were taught under the general heading of 'Technical Studies'.

Four girls, wearing their striped summer uniforms, preparing another culinary delight in this 1960s cookery lesson. From left to right: Ruth Bingham, Joy Williams, -?-, -?-. Mrs Jean Grasby, head of housecraft, was a cookery teacher at the time of this photograph. During the period when the school didn't have its own cookery classrooms and kitchens, pupils were taken by bus to, firstly, Henbury School and latterly Monk's Park School to use their facilities for cookery lessons.

Mr John Chater takes a chemistry lesson in 1970 in one of the rooms attached to the library in the sixth-form block. From left to right: Robert Head, of Burke House, who attended the school between September 1963 and January 1971, John Jefferies, Ian ? and Stephen Buston.

A lesson in the physics laboratory, c.1970. The girls seated at the table on the left, engaged in great merriment rather than study, are, from left to right: Elaine Shore, Ann Curtis, Yvonne Bishop, Sarah Dawes, Linda Evans. The boys seated are, from left to right: Andrew Bevington, Dennis Alford, Martin Davis. John Griffin is standing. The two girls seated on the far right of the picture are Susan Ashfield (writing) and Susan Hayward.

Head of art, Mr Reg Batterbury, demonstrating to a group of pupils what appears to be a small old printing press with typesetting paraphernalia evident on the worktop. Judging by the style of uniform this picture was taken within a year or two of the school opening in 1954. David Butler is the pupil looking over Mr Batterbury's shoulder.

The skeleton of mammals is the subject of Mr Crowe's 4.1 biology class in school year 1969-70, as the anterior view of a lumbar vertebra on the blackboard illustrates. It is believed that the girl with the ribbon in her hair is Kathleen Wollacott; Catherine Jones is seated front left. Carol Frampton appears more interested in the cameraman than mammalian bones!

Ann Davey, nearest the camera, and Pauline Dursley are a picture of concentration during their typing lesson, c.1970. They would have been working towards a RSA (Royal Society for the encouragement of Arts, Manufactures & Commerce) typing qualification. The classroom, located in Burke House, had specially designed desks that when opened revealed the manual typewriter. Mr Crabbe taught commerce and typing in this room in the 1960s and 1970s. The poster on the wall extols the virtue that 'Clear and Correct Addressing Speeds Your Mail!'

An art lesson in one of two art rooms located on the upper floor of the science block, c.1969. At the time, the art teacher providing tuition was Mr Reg Batterbury, who exhibited his pictures at the annual Royal West of England Art Academy shows in Queens Road. Shirley Evans is second from the left, with the then fashionable feather-cut hairstyle, with Colleen O'Brien fourth from the left. Jill Hedges, is on the opposite side of the table, looking up.

A page from the Commemoration Day Programme for the distribution of certificates and awards, dated Thursday 6 January 1972. The principal guest that evening was R.W. Bolland, director of Bristol Polytechnic. As well as recording pupils' academic achievements during the school year 1970-71, the programme also included results of house competitions. Burke won the Work and Conduct Championship for the year with 6,252 points, beating Fry into second place, Beaufort were third and Cabot fourth. Cabot won the games championship for the year. The school records at one time were recorded in the school magazine, but from edition number nine the magazine was entirely devoted to literary work and the school records were transferred to the Commemoration Day Programme.

An interesting comment in the programme is that Laurence Lloyd, who attended the school between 1960 and 1965, was selected on several occasions to play for the English Association Football Team. He won a number England Amateur under-eighteens caps just after leaving school.

G.MES COMPETITION - RESULTS

	1	2	3	4
Athletics:				
Sports Day	Cabot	Burke	Fry	Beaufort
Standards	Cabot	Burke	Fry	Beaufort
Basketball	Fry	Cabot	Burke	Beaufort
Chess	Beaufort	Cabot	Burke	Fry
Cricket	NO COMPETITION			
Cross-Country	Fry	Burke	Beaufort	Cabot
Netball	Beau. & Burke equal first.		Cabot	Fry
Rounders	Cabot	Beaufort	Burke	Fry
Rugby	Fry	Cabot	Beaufort	Burke
Soccer	Fry	Cabot	Burke	Beaufort
Swimming	Cabot	Burke	Beau. & Fry equal third.	
Tennis	NO COMPETITION			
Hockey	Cabot	Burke	Beaufort	Fry

GAMES CHAMPIONSHIP FOR THE YEAR

1.	CABOT	(140 pts.)	3.	FRY	(102 pts.)
2.	BURKE	(110 pts.)	4.	BEAUFORT	(88 pts.)

MAJOR AWARDS

Head Girl's Award	...	...	...	MAUREEN JAY
Head Boy's Award	...	...	...	DAVID RENNOLDS

Most praiseworthy result in Public Examinations:

R.A. Fenn Cup	...	...	...	DAVID DEAS

In recognition of loyalty and service not otherwise rewarded:

Littlejohns Cup	...	...	...	CATHERINE JONES
McLaren Cup	...	...	...	NIGEL CROWDER

Most praiseworthy Athletic Achievement:

S. J. Adams Cup	...	...	...	CARVIE CURRIE

For Community Social Service:

Wadham Cup	...	...	...	CATHERINE PARKINSON

Public Speaking:

Eunice Bennett Cup	...	...	...	NORMA WILLIAMS

French:

Linda Davidge Cup	...	...	...	CATHERINE JONES

Larry Lloyd, pictured in 1969, made his England debut aged twenty-two years and 224 days against Wales at Wembley on 19 May 1971, in a Home Championship match that ended in a 0-0 draw. He played a second time for his country that year at Wembley on 9 November against Switzerland in a European Championship Qualifier that resulted in a 1-1 draw. Larry attended Lockleaze Secondary School prior to beginning his professional football career with Bristol Rovers. Hometown club Rovers accepted a £50,000 bid for Lloyd in the April of 1969 with manager Bill Shankly looking for a long-term successor to ageing skipper and defender Ron Yeats. After 150 appearances for Liverpool and a brief interlude with Coventry City, Larry joined Nottingham Forest in 1976 for what was to become the most successful period of his football career. In 1979, Lloyd and Forest, under Brian Clough, won the European Cup and retained the League Cup, before amazingly retaining their European crown in 1980. Also that year, Lloyd earned a recall to the England squad and played in the 4-1 defeat to Wales in the Home Internationals. It was to be his fourth and final cap, coming eight years after his previous one.

John Bennett and Reggie Smart assist a fellow pupil to put up a poster in the geography classroom, *c.*1969. Susan Studley (left) and Shirley Davis are the two girls seated at the desk.

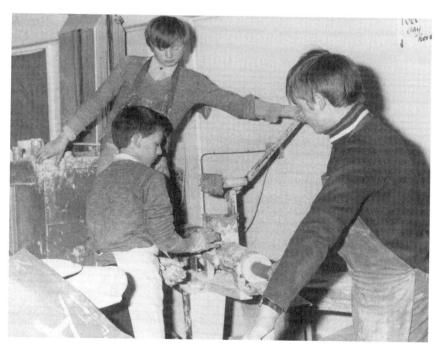

Michael Thomas is the boy about to pull the lever of the clay-forming machine during a pottery lesson in Mr Bernie Johnson's pottery room during the late 1960s. Miss Paula Hubner first taught pottery as a subject at the school. Perhaps overalls rather than aprons would have been more beneficial in helping to protect the boys from the effects of wet clay and wet-clay fights.

The fishpond, built in the 1960s, was located on the lawn outside 'Rainbow Alley' and adjacent to the window of what was then general science room one. Mr Dick Farr, a science teacher, organised pupils to dig the garden for the formation of the new pond.

The pupils appear very studious in this fourth form class, *c.*1968. Sitting at the row of desks nearest the wall are, from left to right: -?-, -?-, Colin Dibbins, Andrew Walters, Leslie Lloyd, Timothy Osborne and Steven Jeremiah (sucking his pen). Geoffrey Dunn is seated at the back. Patricia Weaver and Anne Savage are both concentrating on their writing in the foreground with Mike Slade wearing glasses and Alan Dibbins behind them.

Daily readings being taking from the school's Stevenson's screen instrument shelter, which was sited on the grass area between the main entrance to the building and the school entrance in Hogarth Walk. The medium-size screen was designed to hold maximum and minimum thermometers and a pair of thermometers, one wet bulb and one dry bulb, to create a hygrometer. Stevenson's screens, invented by Thomas Stevenson the father of author Robert Louis Stevenson, were used to shield instruments against rainfall and direct heat radiation from outside sources. The screen allows air to circulate and provides a uniform environment in relation to the air outside the screen. The boy on the right is taking readings from the instruments, whilst his fellow budding meteorologist records the figures. The rain-gauge apparatus sits on top of the screen.

Class 5.2 boys, all of whom wear their prefects tie, pose for a photograph in the physics laboratory in 1970. The picture was taken by physics teacher, Miss Rose Watts (now Mrs White), a year after she commenced teaching at Lockleaze. Around the desk from left to right: Regan Toomer, Nicholas Lanceley, Roy Stone, Ian Haddrell, Adrian Rogers. Standing behind: Marcus Sanyasi, Gerald Holcombe.

This extract is taken from the author's first-year school report – class 1L. At the time classes were designated L, O, C, K, E and A, based on the letters of the name of the school. The report book commenced in the first year and continued throughout the pupil's school life. Education at secondary modern schools focused on training in basic subjects such as arithmetic, mechanical skills such as woodworking and domestic skills such as cookery. In an age before the advent of the national curriculum, the specific subjects taught were chosen by the individual school. As well as the subject teacher's remarks, the house tutor and headmaster, Mr Langley, commented on the pupil's progress. The report also records the number of merits, demerits and any detentions imposed.

Members of the school's Wheatsheaf Club, 1962. From left to right: Linda Freeth, Peter Beavis, Barbara Burleton, Raymond Howell, Mary Edbrooke, David Weedon, Christine Badman, Hazel Betty, Lorraine Gibbard, Tony Godfrey. The club, which started in 1958 as an after-school organization where boys and girls took part in the Duke of Edinburgh's award scheme, was managed by Mr W.T. Baker, and provided activities such as table tennis, country and ballroom dancing, snooker, music, archaeology, cards, cookery, basketball, woodwork, metalwork, netball, first aid, and a young farmers' club. An interesting comment by headmaster Dr Littlejohns writing in 1959 was, 'This type of club is the best answer to the Teddy Boy problem …'

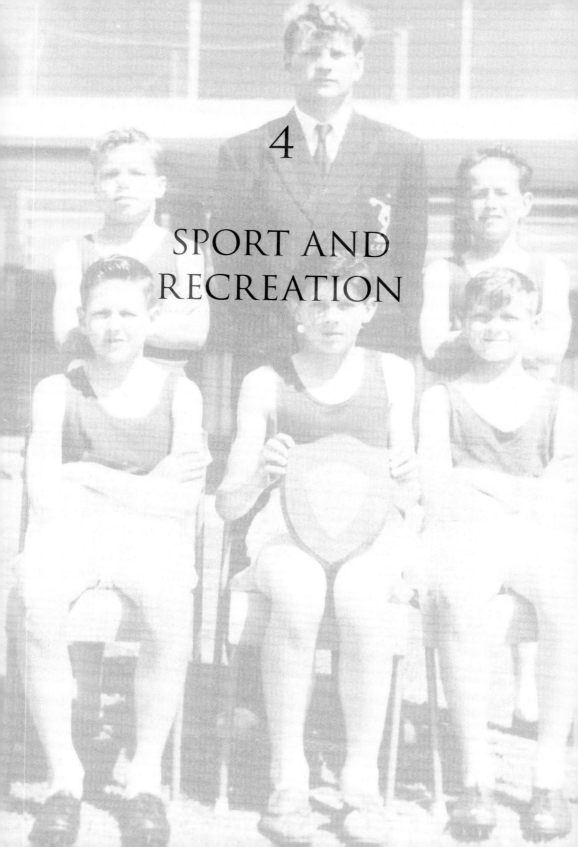

4

SPORT AND RECREATION

Sports day in the early 1960s. The winner of this girls' race is about to pass the finish tape, one end of which is held by the boy with his back to the camera – no sophisticated electronic timing devices at this time.

Senior boys participate in a middle-distance race during the annual school sports day. The weather appears not too warm, as the spectating boys are wearing their blazers. The playing field perimeter fence is on the left and in the distance, with two long barrows just visible on the Purdown horizon.

Parents and pupils watch the finish of a girls' middle-distance race in the 1960s. The tennis courts are immediately behind the spectators with the science block, constructed 1958-59, in the background.

A close finish to the first year boys' 100-yard sprint, as the winner breasts the makeshift tape, in this 1960s sports day race. At this time about 20 acres of ground adjacent to the school were available for games, training and athletics. The houses in the distance are at the top end of Romney Avenue.

Athletics day, summer 1955. Mike Wall, aged eleven, clears 4ft 1in to win the high-jump competition and set a new school record for the event. Roger Farr is the boy standing by the somewhat rudimentary high jump, with John McQuaid in the background.

The high-jump apparatus is now a little more sophisticated than that shown in the previous photograph. History teacher Mr Mervyn Hughes adjudicates during the competition as the girl competitor successfully clears the bar using the simple scissors-style technique.

A fine summer's day, for both spectators and competitors, as Peter Edmunds executes his leap during the boys' long-jump competition during an early-1960s school sports day. Mr Neil Bartle is the teacher standing in the line of pupils. The school's science block is the building on the right, with the houses of Hogarth Walk in the distance.

A competitor in the discus competition showing fine technique. In addition to the annual sports day, pupils took part in the inter-house athletics 'standards' competition, which provided an opportunity for the vast majority of students, whatever their sporting ability, to attain points for their house. Points were awarded to all individual entrants based on their 'standard' against predetermined standards for each athletics discipline. For non-sporty pupils this exercise was probably something akin to purgatory!

Members of Fry House athletics team, probably the boys sprint relay team, display a trophy, c.1961. The teacher is Mrs Gillian Pittard, physical education teacher and Fry housemistress. From left to right: Philip Bevan, Mohammed N. Haq, Michael Richardson, Alan Brown.

Another school athletics team proudly display a shield won in 1956. From left to right, back row: Patrick 'Nobby' Clark, –?–. Front row: –?–, David Richardson, Paul Brookman. Mr Terry Allen is the PE master.

Action from a doubles badminton match taking place in the girls' gymnasium in 1970. Maureen Jay, head girl 1970-71, is the player on the left, this side of the net, her partner is unidentified. Their opponents are Helen Osbon (left) and Susan Loud (right).

Local rivals St Thomas More RC School are the opponents in the weightlifting competition taking place in the boys' gymnasium in 1970. Gareth Lewis is executing the 'clean and press' technique, one of three weightlifting events practiced at the time. Carvie Currie, removing his tracksuit, prepares for his lift.

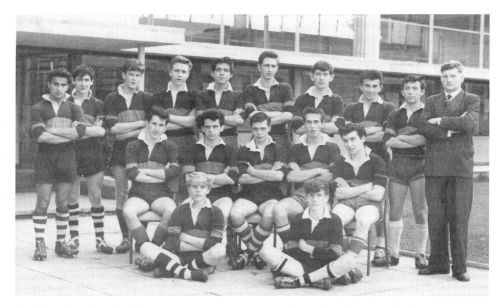

Lockleaze School under-fifteen rugby team, 1960-61. From left to right, back row: Mohammed N. Haq, Richard Hiles, Josh Brown, Ernie Hacker, Billy Williams, Roger Fenn, Robert Beynon, David Cox, Nigel Bly, Mr Terry Allen (PE teacher). Middle row: John Grinter, Peter Edmunds, Richard Hutton, Raymond Edmonds, Raymond Bailey. Front row: David White, David Sloggett. During the season the team played thirteen games, winning nine and losing four; Bailey and Beynon represented Bristol Boys.

The under-fifteen football team reached the final of the Woodcock Shield in 1971. The match was played at the Douglas Ground, Kingswood against Merrywood School, who won the game 3-1, the only goal for Lockleaze being scored by Tony Routledge. From left to right, back row: Terry Sherman, Andrew Priddy, Roger Harper, John Wheeler, Robert Wilkey, Andrew Kirby, Glenn Marshall. Front row: Doug Smith, Steven Bevan, Martin Peacock, Martin Davis, Tony Routledge, Raymond Fielding.

Action from the staff/sixth form verses pupils rugby match taking place in the Dings playing field, *c.*1972. Lockleaze School rugby colours were black shirts with a broad red hoop. Stanley Farm in the distance was a familiar site to all those who played sport in the Dings playing field.

The combined sixth form and staff rugby fifteen at the end of their match against the school fifteen. From left to right, back row: Chris Meechan (art), Peter Radford (English and PE), Neil Milsom (pupil), Bill Lowe, Gary Baker (science), –?–, Graham Lees (woodwork and technical drawing), 'Banger' Hughes (pupil), ? Chan (pupil), Paul Roberts (head of PE). Front row, all pupils: –?–, Andrew Clarke, –?–, –?–, –?–. This picture was taken not long after Paul Roberts commenced his teaching career at Lockleaze in 1972.

The first-year basketball team outside the school's main entrance in 1955. No designer trainers for these lads, just good old-fashioned 'daps'! From left to right, back row: Peter Edmunds, Michael Dawes, Mr Terry Allen (PE master), Reginald Prestidge, Geoffrey Radford. Front row: Roger Harman, John Walters, Michael Wall (captain), George Hunt, Peter Prewett.

Gareth Lewis, wearing the hooped shirt, is the early pace maker at the start of a cross-country race, c.1970. Michael Merrick, Keith Smith, Andrew Kirby, Neil Jones, John Cooper, David Evans, Stephen Harris, Clive Smith and Jeffrey Hancock are other participants heading out of the school playing-field entrance in Romney Avenue.

From left to right: Noel Beresford, David Peters, –?–, Neil Jones (striped shirt), David Rennolds, Martin Painter, Christopher Kendall and Steven Bevan bring up the rear as the runners head off towards Long Wood and Hermitage Wood on Purdown, the course taking them on a circular route to Filton Road and back via Stanley Farm. There was no MOD complex, no dual carriageway and no Hewlett Packard in 1970; mostly open fields and narrow roads.

The runners are back in the school playing field at the end of their cross-country exertions. Martin Painter, Jeffrey Hancock, Andrew Kirby, Martin English, Noel Beresford and Clive Smith all seemed to have survived the ordeal! Tony Evans is the non-participating pupil in school uniform. The sixth-form block is the building beyond the tennis courts.

Not a school photo, but this picture of Manor Farm Boys' Club under-sixteen football team, taken on Horfield Common in 1971, contains ten Lockleaze pupils. From left to right, back row: Cornelius Connelly, Raymond Fielding, Keith Smith, Jeffrey Hancock, Mike Powell, Reggie Smart, Roger Harper. Front row: George Bayliss, Ian Haddrell, Antony Hiscox, Tony Billing, John Fisher. Connelly and Powell did not attend Lockleaze. Season 1970-71 was a particularly successful season for the team, winning the Federation of Boys' Club league and cup competitions.

Under the guidance of Colin Evans, head of mathematics, Lockleaze had a successful school chess team in the 1950s and 1960s. The school entered teams in the *Sunday Times* national chess knockout competition, started in 1958, which involved playing matches by telephone when opponents were some distance away. This is probably one such match from the 1959 season, when the team reached the zone final losing to St Illtyds, Cardiff in a close match. Left to right: Nicholas Sloper, David Richardson, Terry Hill, Geoffrey Radford, Tony Pitson and Roger Fenn – who was selected to play for the England Junior Team.

The girls' first XI hockey team, 1960–61. From left to right, back row: Pamela Cole, Christine Farrant, Christine Grose, Miss Christine Brown (PE teacher), Annette Cheesewright, Linda Davidge, Ann Lyons. Front row: Sandra Quartley, Maureen Kellett, Vera Thomas, Suzanne Brenack, Carol Draper. Despite playing only one game that season colours were awarded to: Annette Cheesewright, Linda Davidge, Christine Grose, Maureen Kellett, Sandra Quartley, Pamela Cole and re-awarded to Suzanne Brenack.

The sixth-form girls' hockey team, in St Trinian's attire, 1973-74, Every year, just before Christmas, the teachers were challenged to a hockey game by the pupils. From left to right, back row: Caroline Bryant, Liz Coltman, Hilary Eustace, Martina Moore, Teresa Purkis. Middle row (kneeling): Gillian Smalldridge, Sheila Hill, Sonia Thompson, Linda Pike. Front row (sitting): Liz Cox and Susan Weston.

Fry House sports team 1960, which came first in the athletics competition with 120 points. From left to right, back row: Raymond Edmonds, David Maddocks, Terry Lewis, ? Brown. Third row: Miss Christine Brown (PE teacher), –?–, Jacqueline Jefferies, Vera Thomas, Valerie Bray, June Gillard, Christopher Parrott, Billy Williams, David Woolford, Philip Shaddick, Mr I.E.A. Evenden, Mr W.T. Baker, Mr R.A. Nicholas. Second row: Maureen Shepherd, Judith Archer, Rachel Adams, Christine Farrant, Sheila Jenkins, Lorraine Slade, Raymond Whittle, –?–. Front row: –?–, Christine Grose?, Patricia White, Susan Davis, Sally Bailey, Eileen Gibbs, –?–, –?–, –?–, William Skuse, Gerald Critchley.

Cabot House sports team were runners–up in 1960. From left to right, back row: Dennis Attwood, Robert Beynon, John Lacey, Henry Shearing, Tony (?) Parry, Roger Pritchard, Roger Fenn. Third row: Mrs D.I. Butterworth, Miss E.M. Bennett, Roger Horsham, Anthony Hutton, Paul Shattock, ? Edmonds, Richard Mills (?), –?–, –?–, Mr K. A. Williams. Second row: Mr J.P. Rosling, Shirley Wood, Janet Conibear, Hilary Gibson, –?–, Celia Slowley, Suzanne Brenack, Judith Isles, Ann Lyons, Mr C. B. Evans. Front row: Valerie Thomas, –?–, –?–, Joyce Searle, –?–, ? Oliver.

Carol Dowling, in front, and Barbara Critchley, who both started at Lockleaze in 1956, photographed by metalwork teacher Mr Oldham at the school sports day in 1961. Mr Oldham's daughter, Rosemary, was a pupil at Lockleaze School between 1959 and 1963.

The Revd Leslie Jones, vicar of St Marys' Church, Gainsborough Square, aided by the headmaster Dr Littlejohns, presents the trophies and prizes at the culmination of the school sports day, in the summer of 1961. Fry House has been triumphant on this occasion, winning with ninety-eight points. Mr Eric Brown, left, and Mr Reginald Cox are the two masters seated at the officials' table, being the scores recorders, announcers of events and results, and providing a commentary over the public address system. Mr David Brown (PE teacher) stands immediately behind them, with Mr John Adams, Mr John Trenchard, Mr David Powell and Mr John Nagle also in the picture.

Fry House sports team proudly display two sports trophies, *c.*1962. Fry won the athletics competition three years in succession from 1960 to 1962. From left to right, back row: -?-, -?-, -?-, -?-, Alan Brown, Mrs Jean Grasby, Mr David Powell. Middle row: Michael Richardson, Virginia Walding, -?-, -?-, Patricia Hodder, Martyn Bryant, Mohammed N. Haq, Andrew Davis, Colin Brittan, -?-, -?-. Front row: -?-, -?-, -?-, -?-, -?-, -?-, -?-, Eileen Gibbs, Mrs Gillian Pittard, -?-, -?-, -?-, ? Carter, -?-, -?-.

The school was divided into four houses, Beaufort, Burke, Cabot and Fry, taking their names from those associated with Bristol. Edmund Burke, 1729-1797, politician, philosopher and polemicist, was MP for Bristol for just six years, from 1774 to 1780; John Cabot (Giovanni Caboto), 1450-1498, a Venetian navigator and explorer commonly credited as one of the first early-modern Europeans to land on the North American mainland in 1497 aboard the *Matthew*, which set sail from Bristol; Elizabeth Fry (née Gurney), 1780-1845, a Quaker philanthropist who pioneered for higher nursing standards and the education of working women. She married Joseph Fry a member of the Fry's Chocolate family; Beaufort House takes its name from the local aristocratic family, whose residence is Badminton House in Gloucestershire. The Beaufort family owned Purdown, including the site of the school, as part of their estate from the 1700s until 1850. Henry Somerset, 1900-1984, the 10th Duke of Beaufort held the office of Lord Lieutenant of Bristol, Lord High Steward of Bristol, Tewkesbury and Gloucestershire, Lord Lieutenant of Gloucestershire and was chancellor of the University of Bristol from 1965 to 1970. He was president of Bristol Rovers Football Club from 1949 until his death on 5 February 1984.

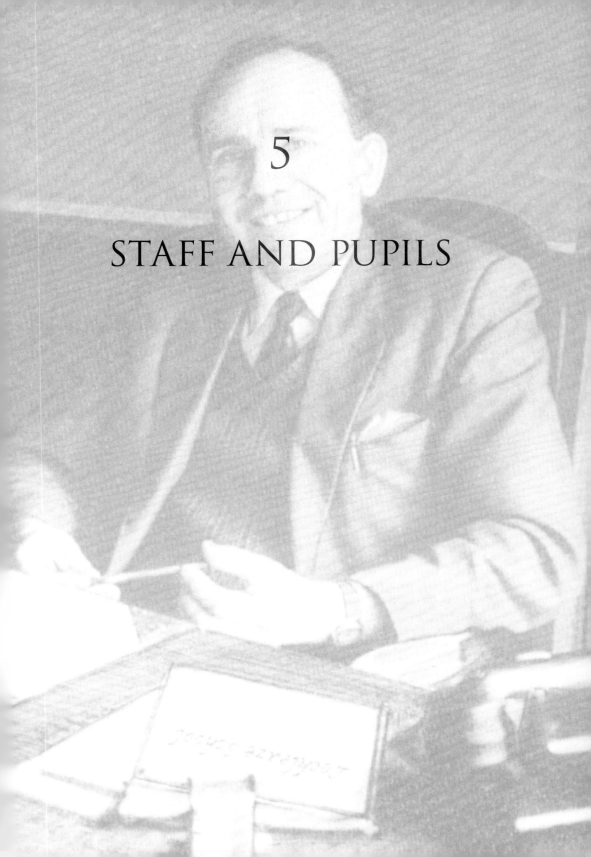

5

STAFF AND PUPILS

This photograph of Lockleaze School staff was probably taken as a memento for headmaster Dr W.N. Littlejohns (seated in the front row) prior to him leaving the school in 1962. From left to right, back row: Mr Kenneth Howell (director of music), Mr D.W. Eneas (mathematics), Mr John P. Rosling (physics), Mr Eric S. Brown (music), Mr John B.J. Martin (housecraft), Mr Derek L. Kerwood (technical studies), -?-, Mr Mervyn Hughes (history), Mr Reginald J. Batterbury (head of art), Mr David J. Brown (physical education), Mr David G. Powell (technical studies), Mr Kenneth A. Williams (head of educational guidance), Mr Dennis C. Sinclair (chemistry), Mr Duncan C. Gordon (German), Mr R.A. Nicholas (head of languages and sixth-form master), Mr Orby F. Crabbe (commerce and typing), Mr Michael J. Perry (head of science). Middle row: -?-, -?-, Mr William J. Baker (mathematics), Mr Lindsay K. Beacham (technical studies), Mr John W. Trenchard (geography), Mr Neil J. Bartle (rural science), Mr K.A. 'Jim' Edwards (deputy headmaster), Mr Terry M. Allen (head of physical education), Mr Colin Evans (head of mathematics), Mr John Adams (head of English), Mr Roger D. Stenner (chemistry), Mr Keith Perry (history), Mr John A. Eastman-Nagle (mathematics), Mr Reginald S.R. Cox (head of religious education), Mr David W. Porter (mathematics), Mr Robert W. Barnes (head of technical studies), Mr O. William Oldham (metalwork). Front row: Jean Angerson (home economics), Miss J. Farrant (English), Mrs Gillian E. Pittard (physical education), -?-, Mrs Glenna R. Paynter (head of geography), Mrs Daisy Butterworth (special needs), Mrs Maureen M. Barnett (French), Miss Paula Hubner (art), Dr William Norris Littlejohns (headmaster), Miss Mary Fay Devaney (science and deputy headmistress), Mrs Jean E. Grasby (head of housecraft), Miss Batt (home economics), Mrs M. Cox (biology), -?-, Mrs O.M.H. Brimson (secretary), Mrs R.A. Loader (secretary), Mrs Edith Ansley (secretary), -?-, Mrs M.W. Sharpe (music).

Members of staff relax in the staff common room in the 1970s. Left to right: Mr R.A. Nicholas (head of foreign languages and sixth-form master), Mr Mervyn Hughes (history), Mr Ken Howell (music), Mr David Archer (mathematics), Bob Milsom, the community policeman. Harveys' Club Amontillado Sherry is the preferred tipple.

Teachers unwind in the common room during a tea/coffee break in 1974. Clockwise from the left: Lynn Elms, Patsy Curtis (geography), Richard Dark (science), Austin Davis (woodwork), James Fagg, Rosla ?, -?- (PE), June Markell (typing), -?- (typing), -?-, -?-, -?-, -?-, -?-, -?-, -?-, Mrs Purnell (history). The view from the window on the right takes in the rooftops of Hogarth Walk, Landseer Avenue and Bonnington Walk playing fields, with Horfield in the distance.

Above: Form 3S pose for a group photograph outside the music room, 1962. From left to right, back row: Alan Hampton, Michael Richardson, Colin Brittan, Gerald Neilson, Paul Morrell, Martin Wilde, Malcolm Carstairs, Alan Brown, Norman Hodges. Middle row: David Treasure, Dennis Rowles, Richard Hook, Owen Morey, Annette Pound, Linda Tuck, Georgina Forse, Marilyn Watkins, Sandra Shepherd, Anne Bryant, Marion Hawker, –?–, Mr B.W. Blackwell, –?–, Robert Thompson. Front row: Joyce Searle, Bonita Hall, Wendy Skidmore, Ann Smith, Linda Hopkins, Pat Morris, Jean Gadsby, Sandra Winter, Patricia Jones.

Opposite above: Form 2A taken in October 1955 outside the main entrance. From left to right, back row: Gerald Churchill, Brian Perry, Howard Tozer, Peter Edmunds, Reginald Prestidge, Geoffrey Slocombe, Duncan Campbell, John Young, Keith Priddle, Keith Veasey. Third row: Tony Pitson, Robert Wilson, Janet Maggs, Jacqueline Cook, Diane Young, Carole Brewer, Gillian Matthews, Judith Lovemore, Brenda Flook, Jennifer Tolley, Joyce Plummer, Roger Fenn, Alan Nash. Second row: Janet Giles, Valerie Wildblood, Diane Heath, Bronwyn Storey, Mr A. Robertson, Mr H.S. Whaley (headmaster), Mr R. S. New, Carole Bennett, Vivian Notton, Susan Davidson. Front row: –?–, Alan Reed, –?–, Thomas Logan.

Opposite below: Mr Nicholas' class of 1958–59, taken inside the school hall where the whole school attended assembly every morning prior to lessons commencing. Grey cardigans are *de rigueur* for the girls. From left to right, back row: John Griffith, –?–, John Rowles, –?–, Tony Godfrey, –?–, Robert Nelmes, Lawrence Edwards, John Pyke. Third row: –?–, John Knight, Lesley Freestone, –?–, Valerie Hurley, Christine Stevens, Maureen Egleton, Carol Billingham, –?–, ? Hemmings. Second row: Lorraine Scull, Patricia Shapcott, Carol Ford, Carol Dowling, Mr R.A. Nicholas, Linda Isles, Barbara Critchley, Patricia Brierley, Sandra Quartley. Front row: David White, –?–, Keith Willis, –?–, –?–, Brian Henson, Christopher Peters, James Brierley.

Pictured in 1962, Fred Langley was born 23 January 1919 at Irthlingborough, Northamptonshire and educated at Wellingborough Grammar School and University College, Nottingham where he obtained a BSc in physics, chemistry and mathematics, and a teaching qualification. His education was interrupted in 1940 by war service. He trained in Rhodesia to become a pilot in the RAF, in which he served until 1946, flying Sunderland Flying Boats on anti-submarine patrols in the North Atlantic. He was awarded the DFM (Distinguished Flying Medal) reaching the rank of Flight Lieutenant, having been promoted from Pilot Officer to Flight Officer in 1944. The DFM was issued to personnel below commissioned rank, for 'an act or acts of valour, courage or devotion to duty whilst flying in active operations against the enemy'. Prior to arriving at Lockleaze he taught at Wellingborough Grammar School, Holt Grammar School, Liverpool, Portsmouth Grammar School, Kimbolton Grammar School, Cambrideshire, Whitley Abbey Comprehensive School, Coventry and then his first headship at Northfields School, Dunstable. He died October 1997, aged seventy-seven.

With a group of pupils in the 1970s, Mr F. Langley, known affectionately to all as 'Fred', served the school as headmaster from 1962 to 1982, being the third of five headmasters appointed during the school's history. Horace Stanley Whaley (1913-1998) 1954-1957, Dr William Norris Littlejohns (1915-1988) 1957-1962, Fred Langley (1919-1997) 1962–1982, Kenneth Williams 1982-1988, and Raymond A. Lockey 1988-2004. Deputy headmistresses included: Miss Mary Fay Devaney (1916-2003) 1954-1970 and Miss Pat Cumming 1970-198?. Deputy headmasters included: Mr A.E. Edwards 1954-1962, Mr R.G. Lacock 1962-1969, Mr John Norwood, Mr John Angle and Mr James Fagg who retired in 1992.

Eighty members of staff in this group photograph taken in front of the girls' gymnasium and 'Rainbow Alley', 1981–82. From left to right, back row: Mr Mervyn Hughes (history), Mr Chris White (PE), Mr Graham Jerrold (English), Mr R.A. Nicholas (head of foreign languages), Mr Mike Haynes (mathematics), Mr Ian Miller (pottery), Mr Chris Meechan (art), Mr John Burr (SEN), Mr John Else (biology), Mr Mike Adams (chemistry), Mr John Grigg, Mr Lionel 'Pip' Voss (English), Mr David Healey (PE), Mr Kenneth Howell (music), Mr Reg Grey (caretaker), Mr Bob Wathen (SEN), Mr Ron Berry (chemistry), Mr Jon Knowler (physics), Mr Terry Pratt (SEN), Mr Graham Lees (metalwork). Third row: Mr Derek Craven (woodwork), Mr Jack Murray (woodwork), Mr Philip Carter (geography), Mr Gary Baker (biology), Mr John Stockwell (art), Mr Neil Bartle (biology), Mr Richard Dark (science), Mr John Trenchard (geography), Mr Paul Hill (RE), –?–, Mr James Fagg (SEN), Mr Ian Telfer (physics), Mr William Baker, Mr David Archer (mathematics), Mr John Dacey (drama), Mr David King (geography), Mr David Porter (mathematics), Mr John Wordley (music), Mr David Griffiths (geography). Second row: Neil Crewe? (woodwork technician), Mr Austin Davis (woodwork), Ruth Brown (school nurse), Miss Diane Silcock (SEN), Mrs Marion Hurst (technician), –?–, Mrs Barbara Gosden, Miss Rosemary Watts (physics), Mrs Pauline Goodacre (biology), Miss Bridget Turner (history), Mrs Sheila Poltock (cookery), Miss Linda Rolfe (PE), Mrs Janet Pearce (PE), Alison Parsons (needlework), Mrs Lynn Elms (SEN), Mrs Mona Liss–Carless (biology), Mrs Jean Fewster (SEN), Kay Grayston, Mrs Pamela Salvidge (SEN), Mrs Audrey Lambert (SEN), Mr Clean Muranda (history and English). Front row: Vicky Gaye, Mrs Margaret Jones (mathematics), Miss Morag McDonald (English), Daphne Bird (typing), Mrs June Markell (typing), Adrienne Stevens (SEN), Miss Beverly Naylor – later Mrs Verwoert (biology), Gillian Holmes (music), Mr John Tully (mathematics), Mr John Angle (deputy headmaster), Mr Fred Langley (headmaster) Miss Pat Cumming (deputy headmistress), Mrs Doreen Hazell (technician), Heather Broome (technician), Mrs Jenny Dunford (needlework), Mrs Pat Hocking (languages), Betty Webber (office staff), Joyce Barnett (office staff), Freda Barron (office staff), Sister Rosemary Weaver (school nurse).

Robert Hemming and Mike Steward are the subjects of this clever optical illusion taken in the school playing field by Heather Plummer with her Agfa camera in the late 1960s. Mike is the 'Lilliputian'.

Head of religious education, Mr Reginald Cox, with his third year class of 1959-60. From left to right, back row: Jack Tye, Christopher Wood, Anthony Hutton, Robert Dunn, Robert Weetch, Barry Conlin, Anthony Robinson, Peter Beavis, Martin Dancy, Terence Britton. Middle row: Rachel Adams, Judith Archer, Linda Godwin, Hazel Betty, Mary Edbrooke, Pamela Cole, Judith Iles, Sandra Pritchard, Marion Wichard-Takle, Carole Brittan, Linda Fermandell, Rosemary Oldham, Mr R.S.R. Cox. Front row: Barbara Burleton, Christine Badman, Marilyn Counsell, Christine Vaughan, Lorraine Gibbard, Veronica Keefe, Christine Farrant, Shirley Wood. The majority of these pupils started at the school in September 1957.

Julie Alford, left, wears the summer uniform, whilst her friend Gillian Smalldridge is dressed in the winter version. Gillian was about to begin her first year at school – Julie was starting her second year – when this picture was taken in the garden of the Smalldridges' house in September 1968. Sandra Button (Form 2F) writing in the 1963 edition of *Beaufort House* magazine, describes the school uniform of the time:

The school colours are red, black and silver. The girls' berets are black with red and white wheatsheaf badges. The boys' caps are black with red crowns with similar badges. The junior girls' winter uniform is grey tunics and white blouses with a tie of school colours. Girls wear black, brown, or red shoes, but white ones may be worn in the summer. In winter grey or red socks, but white for summer. Senior girls may wear grey skirts and white blouses. Prefects wear red ties. In summer junior girls wear red check dresses while senior girls wear red-checked skirts and white blouses, six-form girls are allowed to wear red-striped dresses. Boys' clothes are the same in winter and summer. They wear blazers, grey trousers and pullovers. Black or brown shoes.

Taken from the summer 1963 issue of the school magazine, *The Wheatsheaf*, heads of the school and second prefects with a selection of the school trophies. From left to right: Tony Sleeman (head boy), Angela Baker (head girl), Pearl Edwards and Barry Roberts.

Beaufort five tutor group, 1970–71. From left to right, back row: Gillian Smalldridge, Jacqueline Vinnicombe, –?–, Kevin Merrett, John ?, Keith ?, Brian Trott, Ann Burt, Julie Alford. Third row: Annette Slocombe?, Mark Newman (?), Mark Welsh, Barry Edwards, Tony Williams, Adrian Evans, Julie ?, Elaine Rees (?). Second row: Tony Evans, Judith Watkins, Roslyn Wilmont, Hilary Roberts, Regan Toomer, Elaine Brown, Yvonne Pike. Front row: Christopher Williams, Kenneth James (?).

Beaufort six tutor group, 1969–70. At the back: Robert Stone. From left to right, back row: Ronald Roost, –?–, Martin White, –?–, Philip Cross, Tommy Harper, David Peters, Robert Bullock, Tony Billing, –?–, Peter Williams, Stephen Bennett. Middle row: –?–, Roberta Hook, Carol Brain, –?–, –?–, Stephen Young. Front row: –?–, –?–, –?–, –?–, Mary Smalldridge, Kathleen Wollacott.

Beaufort seven tutor group, 1969-70. From left to right, back row: Ronald Tarrant, Tony Marshall, –?–, Christopher Button, –?–, –?–, –?–. Fourth row: Martin Painter, –?–, Martin English, –?–. Third row: Andrew Caple, Philip Stone, Stephen Bennett, –?–, Michael White, Roger Partridge. Second row: –?– , Jill Hedges, –?–, –?–, –?–. Front row: –?–, Sally Day, Elizabeth Jay, –?–, Ann Davey, Sonia Dixon.

Beaufort eight tutor group, 1969-70. From left to right, back row: Fitzroy Currie, Marcus Sanyasi, Andy Walcott. Fourth row: Glenn Marshall, Neil Greatorex, –?–, Martyn Bailey, Melford Gardner, –?–. Third row: –?–, Mohammed Razaq, –?–, Michael Thomas, Trevor Mead, Philip Pickford, –?–. Second row: Diane Stone, –?–, Catherine Jones, Catherine Parkinson. Front row: Teresa Rendall, Shirley Evans, Sheila Batten, Heather Cox, Annette Gasson, Linda Upton.

A class photograph of pupils who started school in September 1955, taken 1956-57 outside the school gymnasium. From left to right, back row: Mr Eric Brown (music teacher), –?–, –?–, Raymond Dawe, –?–, –?–, –?–, Keith Smith, Hedley Rylett, –?–, David Mitchell. Third row: –?–, Stephen Sweet, Patricia Williams, Lindra Shore, Carol Mapstone, Ann Waltho, Christine Ward, Veronica Cockram, Diane Williams, Diane Smale, Gillian Mills, Roger Pritchard, –?–. Second row: Maureen Worgan, Janet Conibear, Carol Cardinelli, Maureen Archer, Mr H.S. Whaley (headmaster), Miss Glenna Wilkins, who later became Mrs Paynter, Jeannette Bush, Doreen Hale, Gillian Stone, Margaret Sheppard. Front row: Roland Eyres, –?–, –?–, Colin Brittan, –?–, –?–. Do you recognise the famous pupil? At school he was Roger Pritchard, to pop fans he was known as Lee Sheridan, singer with the Brotherhood of Man. Roger sang with the group between 1973 and 1982 and co-wrote the 1976 Eurovision Song Contest winner 'Save Your Kisses For Me'. Roger is standing second from right in the third row.

School prefects, 21 January 1958. From left to right, back row: Robert Wilson, Terry Annette. Middle row: Christine Bye, Carole Lavis, Peter Prewett, Susan Davidson, Roger Fenn, Patricia Weedon, Tony Pitson, Elizabeth Bowles. Sitting: Richard Hutton, Howard Tozer, –?–, John Walters, Dr W.N. Littlejohns, Carole Brewer, Diane Heath, Elizabeth Wilkins, Patricia Plummer. John Walters and Carole Brewer were appointed head boy and head girl in the autumn term of 1957. John left the school at the end of the 1958 summer term, to be replaced as head boy by Duncan Campbell.

A HEAD GIRL REMEMBERS BY CAROLE BREWER

When the letter from the education authorities arrived that far off day in 1954 stating that your daughter would attend Lockleaze Comprehensive School in September, two questions were asked around the dinner table that evening by my parents. What does comprehensive mean? And where is Lockleaze? Forgive our ignorance, but after only living for two years in this vast city, many areas were still foreign to us.

That day in September eventually dawned and in black blazer purchased from Daniel Neals in Queens Road, black beret stiff with the wheatsheaf badge, grey woollen gymslip scratching my legs, I found the right bus to take me to Gainsborough Square, Lockleaze. The bus halted near the fish and chip shop and I followed the other similarly clad pupils past the few shops and Co-op store flanking the square, then the flat roofed houses, along to the entrance of the school gates. Cycle sheds to the left, staff car park at the front of the building and the curved driveway bordering the assembly hall to the playgrounds. What remains with me to this day is the total newness. The building itself with large windows, the gleaming unscuffed floors, the pristine desks and chairs, the untouched textbooks, but most frightening of all, the unknown staff bustling along corridors with black gowns billowing behind them like in flight ravens.

The attendance register was called, only surnames were used and even today I am only able to remember fellow pupils, both girls and boys, by their surnames. First names were only for your close friends. Dinner money for the week was paid, milk monitors were appointed or just chosen at random, lunch was served in the assembly hall and so the first day began. Mention should be made here of the dreaded school dinners. No choice, under-cooked mashed potatoes with dark uncooked lumps, meat from ancient animals reared only for use in schools, one vegetable, the authorities favourite being cabbage. Pudding was 'frog spawn' [tapioca pudding] or rice pudding with one dollop of jam to share amongst twelve or so pupils. But Friday was fish day. Soggy battered fish and even soggier cold chips. The smell, as well as the unpleasant taste, lingered for hours around the building and mouth respectively.

The playing field hitherto had been a corn field and before any use could be made of the field, we spent a lot of time picking up the stones, both large and small. Even after this back breaking exercise, should one be unlucky enough to encounter the ground during a game of hockey the ensuing grazes were a reminder of the field's previous glory. Blue mottled knees clashed violently against our thin red shorts as we chased the hockey ball across the field, more in an effort to keep warm than to win a game. No warm fleeces in those days, just thin cotton polo shirts to keep out the cold wind that always seemed to blow across that barren field. Then the joy of a warm shower, but no soap! This was 1955 and a warm shower was something new, almost unheard of at home. Trying to locate your own towel slung haphazardly amongst so many was a struggle, almost as difficult as trying to keep the little strip of cotton covering your vital parts. However, worst of all was when the outside door swung open and the incoming draught let the prying eyes of the boys scraping mud off their rugby boots in the quadrangle, catch a glimpse of us pink almost naked girls.

Under the very watchful eye of our deputy head and biology teacher, Miss Devaney, girls were occasionally and frighteningly instructed on the rudiments of sex education, but even more frightening were the Monday morning inspections as we filed into the hall at 9.00 am. Any trace of lipstick, or nail polish from the weekend, or even the glimpse of a hooped petticoat, were instantly spotted and the dread of being pulled out of line and told to remove the traces in the girls' toilet before assembly ensured all girls were well scrubbed.

The intake of 1954 and 1955 formed the core of the school and became the first prefects without role models or guidelines, just drawing on our own resources, as we had no seniors to call on. White belts for the girls and now grey berets to be worn as prefects: only red belts for those with good deportment. John Walters was the first Head Boy and I was first Head Girl. Now we elite could use the front stairs without fear of being reprimanded. During morning assembly John and I stood beside Dr Littlejohns and Miss Devaney and on many occasions had to read the morning lesson without rehearsal or second thought should no one else be on hand to do so.

Fifty school prefects assemble outside the main entrance in 1961. From left to right, back row: John Grinter, James Climie, Richard Hutton, Anthony Read, Peter Edmunds, Philip Lanceley, Howard Tozer, Tony Pitson, David Richardson, Raymond Edmonds, Gordon Brown, Dennis Attwood, Robert Beynon, Richard Hiles, Tony Sleeman (Beaufort house captain), Christopher Haggett, Ernest Takle, Robin Haggett, Barry Roberts (Fry house captain), Stuart Armsby (Cabot house captain). Middle row: Janet Shorland, Celia Slowley, Janet Green, Linda Davidge (Cabot house captain), Annette Cheesewright, Sonja Forse, Christine Grose, Vera Thomas, Diane Perry, Margaret Lloyd, Angela Baker, Mary Horley, Susan Davidson, Suzanne Brenack, Susan Wallace, Carol Northam, ? Baker, Richard Fletcher. Front row: Beryl Palmer, Beryl Rogers, Lesley Avery, Pearl Edwards (Fry house captain), Roger Fenn (deputy head boy), Duncan Campbell (head boy), Jennifer Tolley (head girl), Carole Lavis (deputy head girl), Jennifer Archer, Joyce Plummer, Jacqueline Hocking, Patricia Gillard. Margaret Lloyd returned to the school, as Mrs Margaret Jones, to teach mathematics.

6

EVENTS

The lord mayor's pair-horse Landau with coachmen stands outside the main entrance to the school in Hogarth Walk. The Landau was built at the turn of the century by the well-known Bristol firm of Fullers at their works in St George's Road on a site behind the present Council House.

Cllr. Claude Draper (1908–2000), a member of the Board of Governors, addresses the assemblage on Gainsborough Square, whilst the Lord Mayor of Bristol, Cllr. William G. Cozens, and headmaster Dr Littlejohns listen to the speech. Cllr. Draper's daughter, Carol, was a pupil at Lockleaze School. The purpose of the lord mayor's visit to Lockleaze is uncertain, however it is suggested that it was associated with ceremonial planting of trees around the centre grass area of the square.

The Lord Mayor of Bristol presents pupils with a memento of his visit in 1960. The girl stood directly in front of the lord mayor is Yvonne Graves, who started at the school in September 1959. Cllr. Draper (back to camera) and headmaster Dr Littlejohns are in attendance. Mr Reg Batterbury, an art teacher at the school, rushes forward to take a photograph of the occasion.

Pupils and their families gather on Gainsborough Square for the event. The boys wear distinctive black and red school caps, the girls black berets. Cllr. Draper wearing a long overcoat, is on the left, with Mr H. Thomas, a history teacher at the school, standing in front of the boy pupils. Jacqueline Harding, Mrs Edna 'Betty' Harding and Mrs Adams stand immediately behind the small girl with bunches in her hair. The top of Constable Road is behind the crowd, with Horfield in the distance.

During May 1958 four Spanish government officials spent two weeks in the United Kingdom as guests of the Foreign Office and under arrangements made by the Central Office of Information. The officials arrived in Bristol on Monday 5 May 1958 on a three-day visit to study local government. The group were greeted by Senor Jorro y Vives, the Spanish Vice-Consul in Bristol, prior to visiting senior officers of Bristol City Council at the Council House.

During their tour the party visited Lockleaze Secondary Modern School, where they saw the pupils at their studies. This photograph shows the Spanish officials being shown one of the school's classrooms by Mr K.A. Edwards, the second master. Boys seated from left to right, back row: Keith Priddle, Roger Fenn. Front row: Tony Pitson, Howard Tozer. Thomas Logan is the boy with spectacles in the centre of the picture; Carol Bennett is the girl looking at the camera, Valerie Wildblood beside her.

The four officials are: Ilmo. Senor Don Luis Rodriguez de Miguel, under-secretary, Ministry of the Interior; Ilmo. Senor Don Jose Maldonado Fernandez del Torco, under-secretary, Ministry of Education; Ilmo. Senor Don Juan Ortiz Gracia, technical secretary-general, Ministry of Finance, and Ilmo. Senor Don Jesus Fueyo Alvarez, national delegate of the press, propaganda and radio in the Ministry Secretariat-General of the Movement. Carol Bennett and Valerie Wildblood are the pupils.

The party also visited the Lockleaze housing estate, and saw some of the dwellings built by the council. This photograph shows them leaving one of the houses in Bonnington Walk after being received by the resident. Landseer Avenue is in the distance.

A makeshift dais has been erected for Cllr. Robert Wall to address staff and pupils on the occasion, in 1971, of the delivery of the new school minibus. From left to right: Mr Eric Brown (music), Mr Lionel 'Pip' Voss (English), David Rennolds (head boy), Mr Fred Langley (headmaster), Cllr. Robert Wall, Mr Michael Perry (head of science), Maureen Jay (head girl).

Music teacher Eric Brown takes receipt of the keys and log book of the new minibus from Cllr. Robert Wall, a member of the Board of Governors. Sir Robert Wall, as he is now, served as a member of Bristol City Council from 1959, as Leader of the Council during the early eighties, and was leader of the local Conservative Party for over twenty years. He worked in Bristol's aviation industry and authored several works on Bristol history and a history of aviation industry in Bristol.

The whole school assembled in the boys' playground to witness the event. Dinah Hole and Gail Burrows are amongst the crowd of pupils taking a respite from lessons to watch the presentation. Miss Wendy Hateley, one of the girls' sports mistresses, also enjoys the sunshine.

Mr Langley takes the wheel as he prepares to take the dignitaries for a ride in the new school minibus. Mr Martin and Miss Hateley hold back the crowd. The minibus was used for the first time to transport the under-fifteen football team to the Woodcock Shield final at the Douglas Sports Ground, Kingswood.

Science teacher Neil Bartle, who taught at Lockleaze between September 1959 and July 1993, shows the Duke of Edinburgh part of the exhibition in the rural science room during his visit to the Wheatsheaf Club at the school, on 30 October 1959. The lord mayor, Cllr. W.G. Cozens also shows an interest in the display, whilst Mr W.T. Baker, warden of the club, talks to a police dignitary in the background. The duke met over 200 boys and girls of the school's Wheatsheaf Club on his visit, which was made to enable him to see how the award scheme was progressing in Bristol.

Prince Philip inspects a model aircraft made by John Watson (aged fifteen), a member of the Boys' Brigade and pupil at the school. The lord mayor, the secretary of the Bristol Youth Committee, Mr Edward Seath (centre), and Boys' Brigade officer, Lieutenant Ken Sweet (on the left) look on with interest. Outside the school the 50th (Lockleaze) Company of the Boys' Brigade and the Lockleaze Unit of Bristol Red Cross Cadets formed a guard of honour for the duke's visit.

The Duke of Edinburgh pauses to talk to members of the Lockleaze Unit of Bristol Red Cross Cadets as he concludes his hour-long visit to the school. Paula Hubner, an art teacher, chaperones the royal visitor at the temporary campsite set up near the main entrance. The girls cooking sausages and onions over a campfire are kneeling, left to right: Christine Ward, Carole Pegler, Celia Brown, Wendy Harding, Linda Hill. Lindra Shore is the cadet standing.

Prince Philip commented, 'I don't think that the sausages are cooked, except for that one on the end' and he indicated one very well-cooked sausage. He was asked by sixteen-year-old Wendy Harding if he would like one, and the duke replied 'Yes, I'll have that one,' and pointed to the one he had indicated earlier. He was offered a bread roll, but the duke said that he would prefer the sausage on its own on a plate, whereupon Carole Pegler speared the sausage and handed it to him on a tin plate. Taking the sausage in his fingers the duke bit it in half and exclaimed, 'Very good indeed.'

The theme of Lockleaze School's float is the wild west, with an 'uncovered' wagon, Red Indians and salon girls evident. The articulated lorry is about to pull into Gainsborough Square from the top of Bonnington Walk in this 1980s picture.

During a school visit to Bristol Docks a group of boys pose next to a Canadian ship moored in the harbour. The picture must have been taken after 15 February 1965, when the new Canadian flag was inaugurated in Ottawa, as the ship flies the new maple leaf flag to the left of the funnel. The building on the right was the now closed Bristol Industrial Museum on Prince's Wharf.

The school production of Shakespeare's romantic comedy *A Midsummer Night's Dream*. Following six weeks of rehearsals the first performance took place on 19 December 1960. From left to right, standing: –?–, Jeffrey Russell (Bottom), –?–, –?–, John Grinter (Flute), Tony Pitson (Philostrate), –?–, Jennifer Tolley (Hippolyta), –?–, Duncan Campbell (Demetrius), Pearl Edwards (Helena), Howard Tozer (Lysander), Carole Lavis (Hermia), James Climie (Oberon), Anita Sims (Titania), Ann Coles (Puck). Seated are the fairies played by Susan Hillard, Gillian Robinson, Marilyn Ackerman and Ann Pritchard. The other cast members were: Roger Fenn (Theseus), Christopher Haggett (Egeus), Paul Shorland (Quince), Quentin Nichols (Snug), John Grinter (Flute), P.J. Evans (Snout), Ashley Bryan (Starveling).

Chu Chin Chow, a musical comedy written by Oscar Asche with music by Frederic Norton, based on the novel *Ali Baba and the Forty Thieves*, was performed by the school in December 1957. In this scene, 'The Feast', are from left to right, back row: Howard Tozer (Kasim Baba), Rita Griffiths (wine seller), Christine Vaughan (Alcolom), Gillian Matthews, Jeffrey Russell (Zanim), D. Andrews (Mukbill). Front row: Geoffrey Eynon (Sacha), Carole Pegler (Corraline), Mr H. Thomas (Abu Hassan), Carole Brewer (Zahrat), Roger Evans (Persian fanner), Christopher Overton (Persian fanner).

Wendy Annette, held by her mother Olive, kisses her brother Terry goodbye prior to his departure on a school trip to St Malo, France, 27 July 1956. The group, pictured at Stapleton Road Railway Station, wear the original style wheatsheaf badge on their blazers; the boys the original design of school cap. From left to right, back row: Maureen Spence, Jeffrey Donadel, -?-, David Critchley, Joyce Jenkins. Front row: Margaret Sheppard, Maureen Hampton, Terence Hill, James Climie, Christopher Parrott, Diane Perry, Judith Lovemore.

The group of second-year pupils, who started at Lockleaze School in September 1954, are pictured here en route to Southampton to board the ferry *The Fallaise* which conveyed them to Brittany for a ten-day holiday. From left to right, back row: Maureen Spence, Jeffrey Donadel, Terry Annette, -?-, David Critchley, Joyce Jenkins, Angela Pennycad. Front row: Mr R.S. New (senior French master), Maureen Hampton, Margaret Sheppard, James Climie, Terence Hill, Christopher Parrott, Diane Perry, Judith Lovemore, Miss Ann Gregory (PE Teacher).

Jean Gadsby (left) and her twin sister Janet (aged fourteen) parade down the catwalk at a fashion show in the school hall in 1961. They are wearing pink and white candy-stripe pyjamas with lace edging. Spectators seated in the front row from left to right: Lynne Aldus, Pamela Sandy, -?-, Carol Holland, Janet ?, -?-.

The 'model' on the catwalk exhibits to an audience of female pupils the latest fashion clothing and accessories for young ladies. The fashion show took place in the school assembly hall in the 1960s, a period when such events were a regular and popular feature of school life.

The first of Britain's musical passion plays, *A Man Dies* was written by Ewan Hooper – then with the Bristol Old Vic Theatre – and the Revd Ernest Marvin, and produced by members of St James' Presbyterian Church. It became the forerunner to later productions like *Joseph and his Amazing Multicolour Dreamcoat* and *Jesus Christ Superstar*. The picture taken by Reg Batterbury, an art teacher at Lockleaze School who also designed posters for the play, is of a rehearsal at St James' Church hall in 1964, featuring from left to right: David Goddard, John Scotcher, Geoffrey Lewis, Linda Hewitt, Marion Hawker.

A full dress rehearsal of the play in St James' Church hall, March 1960. Christ, played by twenty-one-year-old apprentice Kenneth Maughan, carrying his cross to Calvary is surrounded by teenagers dancing to rock music. The first version of the play was presented in St James' Church hall at Easter 1960. Providing the music are local band 'The True Tones' comprising, from left to right: Michael Gwilliam, Ron Cooper, Richard Smith, Andy Reynolds, Jeffrey Donadel. Smith and Gwilliam co-wrote the music. 'Charlie' Hiscox is the dancer on the left.

Ernie Marvin, at the microphone, directs cast members from the stage at a rehearsal of *A Man Dies* at the Colston Hall in 1966. The musicians on stage behind him are local Bristol band 'Mark Roman and The Javelins'. In 1961 and 1962 the play was presented to a packed house in the West Country's largest auditorium during Holy Week. ABC Television televised an extract from the play lasting three-quarters of an hour, the nativity section produced on *Sunday Break* by ABC in March 1961 under the title *Man in Time*. The published version was produced at the Colston Hall and the Royal Albert Hall, London, in the spring of 1964.

Members of St James' Church in one of the many coaches that travelled from Lockleaze to the Royal Albert Hall for the performance of *A Man Dies* on Tuesday 24 March 1964. Sylvia Cooper, who played Mary, is standing in the aisle, with to her left, Roy Harkness, who played the part of Jesus and Roland Williams who played Joseph. Paul Wootten, who portrayed Peter, is the other cast member standing. The Revd Marvin is seated centre with in front of him Mrs Gladys Strachan, of Romney Avenue, a helper at the church.

Columbia Records released a record in 1964 of the songs from the play in 1964, depicting Roy Harkness as Christ on the album cover. Ken Scott reviewing the album in the *Archivist* had this to say:

A Man Dies is an attempt to present the Bible story in the modern idiom – in the music and dancing which teenagers love so much and can do so well. This is definitely an electric album and it's got the early UK 1960s written all over it. The main performers are identified as Valerie Mountain, Ricky Forde and a group called The Strangers (with the boys and girls of St James', Lockleaze). Swinging pop, jangly beat, slow blues rock, Hard Days Night-era Beatles, talk-singing over a beat – it's all here spanning twenty-six tunes that feature titles like 'How Long, Lordie?', 'Do Us A Favour', 'What's The Use?', 'Look In The Paper', 'Ding Dong', 'Riding On A Donkey', 'Who Is My Neighbour?', 'Gentle Christ', etc. Even a couple of surfy twangin' instrumentals in classic Ventures/Shadows tradition ('Dominator' and 'Jack Knife'). No keyboards from what I can tell – just revved-up drums, bass and raw electric guitars. Cover says it was first performed in 1960. I'm surprised this isn't more widely known, especially given that it's on a major label. Seldom has early Jesus music sounded so alive and bursting with energy as it does on *A Man Dies*.

The film *Some People*, made by Vic Films and directed by Clive Donner, provided an excellent window into 1962 British working-class teenage culture, despite being a corny propaganda film for a British social engineering policy programme of the 1960s. Bert (David Hemmings), Bill (David Andrews), and Johnnie (Ray Brooks) are a trio of juvenile delinquents in Bristol who lose their driver's licences after a 100mph accident on their motorcycles. Bored without their speed machines and alienated in their economically depressed factory town, they assemble a rock band with the aid and encouragement of Mr Smith (Kenneth More), the choir director of a local church who offers his facilities for rehearsal space. The band becomes involved with a youth awards programme devised as a community outreach vehicle by the Duke of Edinburgh and the British government, and despite some lingering moments of dissension, they begin to turn their lives around, encouraged all the while by a hopeful adult community. There is some nice Bristol location footage in the film, including the BAC factory, the Clifton Suspension Bridge, the Water Tower Café on Durdham Downs, and scenes in St Mary's Church and church hall, Landseer Avenue, Gainsborough Square and Constable Road, Lockleaze. The interior shots of Johnnie's home were filmed in a house in Landseer Avenue. The film starred Kenneth More, Ray Brooks, David Hemmings, David Andrews, Angela Douglas, Fanny Carby, Harry H. Corbett, Richard Davis, Frankie Dymon, Michael Gwynn, and Annika Wills. Angela Douglas's singing voice was dubbed by Valerie Mountain who with the Eagles released a 45 rpm EP of the soundtrack.

Taken outside the Tate Gallery during a class trip in 1959. The group also did some sightseeing in the capital having travelled to London by train. Pupils from left to right: Barbara Burleton, Christopher Wood, -?-, Judith Archer, Shirley Wood, Martin Dancy. The art teachers are Mr Reg Batterbury and Miss Paula Hubner.

A party of chiefs and legislators from the mid-western region of Nigeria visited the secondary school in November 1965. The party comprised: The Honourable Patrick Kaorhorhiebe Tabiowo, Speaker of the mid-western House of Assembly; H.H. Samuel Usifo Enoseghe II, the Onogie of Ewohimi; Chief Uaman Lawal Osula, the Arala of Benin; H.H. Obi Raymond Umejei Onyetenu, the Asagba of Asaba; Federal Senator Chief Edmund Edun Boyo, the Olutse of Jakpa. The visitors listen to science teacher, Mr Neil Bartle, instructing pupils in a biology lesson in general science room one.

Chris Meechan, an art teacher, ran the caving club at Lockleaze School, which was mainly for sixth-form pupils. Chris (with beard) is pictured with a group from the club outside Goatchurch Cavern, Burrington Combe in 1974. One of the girls is thought to be Sally Gingell. The caving club visited most of caves in the Mendip Hills, leaving school at around 4 p.m. in the school minibus usually driven by Chris, and sometimes returning at around midnight.

The Caving Club was an off shoot of the Wheatsheaf Club and held its first meeting in the summer of 1962 in one of the school classrooms. Roger Stenner, a science teacher, organised the club as he was a member of the Bristol Exploration Club and there were a handful of pupils involved at the start, including: Gerald 'Jock' Neilson, Paul Morrell, David Coombs, Joyce Searle, and teachers Miss Hogarth and Mr Brown.

LOCKLEAZE SCHOOL

40th ANNIVERSARY CELEBRATIONS

To be held as follows:

FOR FORMER STAFF — Friday 31 March 1995, 7.30 pm

FOR FORMER PUPILS & STAFF

Tuesday 4 APRIL 1995, 7.30 pm — 1954 to 1974 (1st 20 years)
Thursday 6 APRIL 1995, 7.30 pm — 1974 to 1994 (2nd 20 years)

TICKETS

- £3.00 which will include a Buffet (£5.00 for 2/3 nights)
- available from the school by either calling in or sending a s.a.e. with the correct remittance.
- Final numbers need to be known by Friday 24 March 1995

SPREAD THE WORD!

WE WANT TO SEE AS MANY
FORMER PUPILS AND STAFF AS POSSIBLE

Lockleaze School
Romney Avenue
Lockleaze, Bristol, BS7 9XT
Telephone: Bristol 694355
Fax: Bristol 792963

R.A. LOCKEY
Headteacher

Raymond Lockey, the then headmaster, organised a reunion in 1995 for all former pupils and staff to celebrate the fortieth anniversary of the opening of the school. A series of events was held over a number of evenings, with more than 600 former pupils from 1954 to 1974 attending on Tuesday 4 April, to hear the stern tones of an 'assembly' by Fred Langley, headmaster from 1962 to 1982. One hundred members of staff attended the staff reunion held on 2 July 2004 at the Marriott Hotel, College Green. It was open to all teachers who taught at the school between 1954 and 2004.

Lockleaze School reunion, 4 April 1995, pupils whose school entry year was 1958. From left to right, back row: Andrew Chudleigh, Glyn Grainger, David Connelly, Michael Richardson, Martin Bryant, Marion Hawker, Philip Parrott. Middle row: David Morris, Derek Aylesbury, Steve Bull. Front row: -?-, Harlette Preist, Sylvia Cooper, Elizabeth Hill, Marilyn Gray, Paulette Kirby.

Lockleaze School reunion, 4 April 1995, pupils whose school entry year was 1964. From left to right, back row: Gerald Price, Vaughan Allen, Brian Leach, Stephen Dawe. Middle row: Bryan Balson, Linda Knight, Wendy Beake, Helen Osbon, Julia Baker, Susan Buckland. Front row: Sandra Roberts, Christine Thomas, Janice Bailey, Gareth Lewis, Anne Thompson.

Lockleaze School reunion, 4 April 1995, pupils whose school entry year was 1960. From left to right, back row: Martin Brown, Suzanne Priest, –?–. Middle row: Philip (?) Norman, Janet MacKenzie, –?–, 'Sammy' Stride, Elizabeth Woodhouse. Front row: Patricia Jones, Martin Kelly, Agnes Graham, Julie Ashton, Diane Verity, Frances Dawes.

A Lockleaze School reunion held at the University of Bristol social club, 14 November 1992, for pupils who attended the school between 1966 and 1971. Included in this photograph are: Bob Bullock, George Bayliss, Tony Evans, Philip Jones, Melford Gardner, Michael Merrick, Noel Beresford, Michael White, Christopher McGrane, Josephine Conlin, Hilary Roberts, Jacqueline Deas, Catherine Phillips, Diane Stone, Gillian Chaplin, Stephen Dan, Hilary Kirby, Sally Day, Neil Greatorex, Elizabeth Taylor, Deborah Paget, Sandra Williams, Martin Painter, Sally Kirkman, Melita Knowlson, Diane Lovegrove, Regan Toomer, Stephen Harris, John Bennett, Shirley Davis, Martin English, David Peters, Adrian Rogers, 'Joby' Rich, Jane Gaydon, Linda Upton, Andre Kirby, Ian Haddrell.

7

ROMNEY AVENUE
SCHOOLS

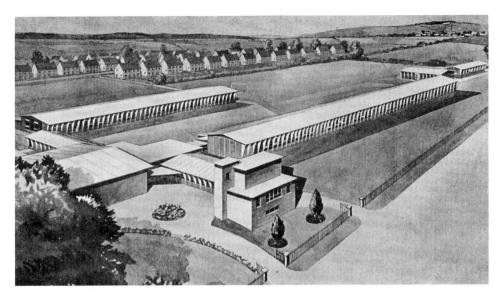

Lockleaze Primary School, Britain's first permanent prefabricated school.

An extract from The Surveyor & Municipal & County Engineer, 18 March, 1949:

Constructed from prefabricated units, developed by the Bristol Aeroplane Co. (Housing) Ltd, in collaboration with the Northern Aluminium Company of Banbury, Lockleaze Primary School was the first permanent prefabricated school to be erected in Britain.

The Lockleaze estate in which it stands consists almost entirely of houses built since the end of the war, and development was so rapid that by the end of 1947 it became imperative to find a speedy method of school construction to meet local educational needs. The solution was found in the new 'Bristol' prefabricated unit system. An order was placed for a twelve-classroom school to accommodate 480 pupils and, within a year of preliminary designs being approved by Bristol Education Committee, the first pupils were admitted. As many of the prefabricated units employed were hand-made, it is confidently expected that, with mass production methods now employed, other schools will be completed in less time.

The layout of Romney Avenue School has been largely dictated by the long and narrow shape of the site of 9½ acres. It is based upon two parallel blocks of seven and five classrooms each, both facing south-east. Focal point of the plan is the entrance hall, off which run the administration and larger classroom block, the connecting corridor to the smaller classroom block, the assembly hall and dining halls. Each classroom has its own cloakroom space with seats and shoe lockers in a recess off the corridor opposite to the room it serves, and each has a large store room. General stock rooms and caretakers' rooms are spaced regularly about the school.

Apart from the entrance, assembly and dining halls, the kitchen and tank tower, all accommodation is of 'Bristol' prefabricated aluminium unit construction. Use of aluminium in this type of structure reduces to a minimum the amount of traditional materials needed and greatly reduces structure weight without loss of strength. Exterior painting is unnecessary, except where colour variety or local harmony is desired, since the material has been tested to withstand all weather conditions.

The buildings were erected complete upon previously prepared concrete rafts. With the exception of some of the roof units, which were partly assembled on site, the sections were delivered from the company's Weston-super-Mare factory complete with internal and external cladding and glazing, so that after erection the only work to be done consisted of laying floor finishes, decorating and installing engineering services and equipment.

Romney Avenue Junior School, built 1948-49 by architects Richard Sheppard and Geoffrey Robson. The prototype of Bristol Aircraft Co.'s Mark I prefabrication system, applied to schools once the need for prefabricated houses was filled. The idea of factory-based construction, using innovative materials like steel and aluminium, started as a way of using spare capacity in factories, such as the BAC, which had been working flat out on the war effort. The row of houses behind the school is Brangwyn Grove.

Everything possible, from the structure and the cladding down to the very doorknobs, was made of heavy-duty aluminium, and everything down to the fins for windbracing was conceived on aeronautical principles. The degree of prefabrication was again high. The walling panels arrived on site entirely made up, with insulation, window frames, and even the glass pre-fixed. For this reason the BAC system, though never cheap, was competitive for primary schools and was widely employed by local authorities before the cost limits started to bite.

Finishing touches being put to the roof in 1949. Because of their aluminium structure the schools, like the bungalows, were confined to a single storey and were therefore suitable only for primary education. Open fields on Purdown stretch into the distance with some newly built houses on Romney Avenue.

This photograph copied from the school's archives shows a completed classroom, c.1949. There were disadvantages with the new system of construction. It was geared to the plain, 'bay' method of classroom planning which dominated British school design for the first few years after the war. Every aluminium school offered the same combination of corridors and classrooms, outmoded educationally and impossible to plan economically in the reduced circumstances of the 1950s.

Some of the original pupils at the new school. The first pupil's name recorded in the Admissions Register of Romney Avenue Junior School was Diane Williams of Romney Avenue, being one of ninety-eight pupils admitted to the school on Monday 7 February 1949. All pupils had previously attended Filton Avenue Infants.

Two girls, one holding her free bottle of milk, look out from the cloakroom at the seven-classroom block of the new school. Ellen Wilkinson as minister of education, the first woman in British history to hold the post, had long been a campaigner against poverty and in 1946 managed to persuade Parliament to pass the School Milk Act. This act ordered the issue of one-third of a pint of milk free to all pupils under eighteen. Harold Wilson's Labour government stopped free milk for secondary school pupils in 1968, and in 1971, Margaret Thatcher, who was Education Secretary under Sir Edward Heath, ended free school milk for children over the age of seven, a move that gave her the nickname 'Thatcher, Thatcher, milk-snatcher'.

Class one, Romney Avenue Juniors, March 1966. From left to right, back row: Christopher Knapp, Andrew Williams, Andre Kirby, Martin Painter, Richard Gurney, Robert Richardson, Tommy Harper, Neil Greatorex, Adrian Rogers, Brian Wadman, David Peters, Ian Gardner. Third row: Elizabeth Taylor, Elizabeth Paul, Kathleen Wollacott, Hilary Kirby, Miriam Sollars, Yvonne Wright, Wendy Annette, Stephanie Pitson, Rachael Dodd, Sandra Williams. Second row: Catherine Jones, Marilyn Hutton, Diane Stone, Josephine Conlin, Mrs D.E. Fahy, Alison Collett, Ruth Nelmes, Valerie Cooper, Shirley Davis. Front row: Barry Riley, Martin English, Colin Hewitt, John Osborne, Ronald Tarrant, David Pike, Roger Partridge.

ROMNEY AVENUE JUNIOR MIXED SCHOOL

LOCKLEAZE, BRISTOL

Report on Conduct and Progress of *Diane Stone.*

Half Year Ending *29th July 1966.* Class *1.*

	REMARKS *Position 5th.*
Arithmetic	*Good work has been done* 90%
English	*Surprising improvement. Good Girl!* 100/120
Reading	*Very good indeed. Good clear voice.*
~~Needlework~~ Handwork	*Very good, careful work.*
Physical Activities	*Very good.*
Other Subjects	*Greek Olympic Games. well done.*
	Played Descant recorder at C. Hall
	Member of School Rounders Team.
Reliability	*Very Good*
Perseverance	*Very Good.*
Speed of work	*Very Good.*

Conduct *Very Good indeed.*

Class Teacher's Remarks *A delightful girl to have in Class 1. is happy, lively and good natured.*

Head Teacher's Remarks *Diane has worked well and made considerable improvement in all work. I am expecting to hear good things of her in her new school* D.E. Fahy

Parent's Signature

130 Edu/8 P&S

Diane Stone's junior school report provides information on her conduct and academic progress, for the half-year ending 29 July 1966. This was Diane's final school report at Romney Avenue prior to moving to Lockleaze Secondary School in September of that year. She finished fifth in Class 1, whose teacher was Mrs D.E. Fahy. An interesting listing under 'Other Subjects' is 'Greek Olympic Games', presumably not now part of the national curriculum!

Romney Avenue Juniors, September 1966 to July 1967. From left to right, back row: John Wheeler, Glenn Marshall, Colin Wilkey, Andrew Kirby, Kevin Merrett, Peter Sheppard, Stephen Fermandell, Peter Randall, Michael Miles, David Adams, Andrew Priddy. Third row: Jane Godfrey, Karen Ellis, Jill Hedges, Martina Moore, Susan Vizard, Madeline Britton, Yvonne Bishop, Heather Cox, Linda Elvins, Colleen O'Brien, Annette Gasson, Teresa Purkis. Second row: Pamela Lewis, Jacqueline Lear, Christine Feltham, Marie Stone, Mrs D.E. Fahy, Toni Edwards, Ann Lewandowski, Mary Tarrant, Elizabeth Cummings. Front row: Daniel Long, David Plumley, Philip Stone, Richard Plumley, Stephen Payne, Peter Wintle, Dennis Alford, Steven Weston.

Romney Avenue Juniors, c.1963. From left to right, back row: Andrew Williams, David Peters, Andre Kirby, Brian Wadman, Tommy Harper, Alan Price, Keith Smith, Martin Painter, Robert Richardson, Adrian Rogers, Barry Nelmes. Third row: Julie Naish, Kathleen Wollacott, Christina Cottrell, Julia Stone, Wendy Annette, Linda Jones, Yvonne Wright, Stephanie Pitson, Ruth Nelmes, Valerie Cooper, Carol Laws. Second row: Shirley Davis, Elizabeth Taylor, Catherine Jones, Rachael Dodd, Josephine Conlin, Mrs Dodd, Elizabeth Jay, Diane Stone, Sandra Williams, Jacqueline Deas, Sheila ?. Front row: Ronald Tarrant, John Osborne, David Pike, Christopher Knapp, Mark Leonard, Martin English.

Romney Avenue Junior School netball team, c.1966. From left to right, back row: Jane Pavey, –?–, Stephanie Pitson, Susan Slade, Wendy Annette, Pauline Williams. Front row: Valerie Cooper, Pauline Wheeler, Jane Vickerman, Margaret Hook, Rosemary Hobbs.

Romney Avenue Junior School netball team, c.1966. From left to right, back row: Alison Collett, Josephine Conlin, Kathleen Wollacott. Middle row: Ruth Nelmes, Stephanie Pitson, Yvonne Wright, Miriam Sollars, Wendy Annette, Valerie Cooper, Miss Hughes. Front row: Catherine Jones, Elizabeth Taylor, Diane Stone, Sandra Williams, Shirley Davis.

Romney Avenue Junior School chess club, *c.*1966. Standing: Diane Stone (left) and Valerie Cooper. Seated clockwise: Robert Richardson, Brian Wadman, Barry Riley, Christopher Knapp, David Pike, John Osborne.

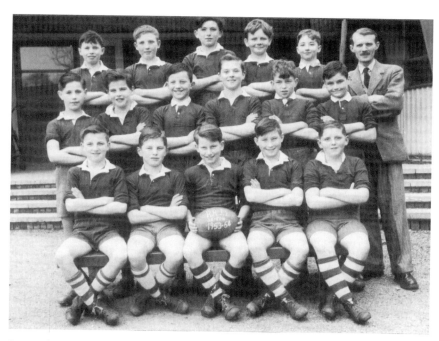

Romney Avenue Junior School rugby team, 1953–54. From left to right, back row: Mike Wall, Peter Galsworthy, -?-, Gerald Gillard, Desmond Tippins, Mr Davies. Middle row: -?-, James Reynolds, Brian Gazzard, Clive Bennett, John McQuaid, Robert Allen. Front row: Mike Dawes, John Walters, Bobby Isaacs (captain), Peter Prewett, David Fitzgerald.

Romney Avenue Junior School football team, champions of Junior League D, 1967–68. The teacher is Mr Elton Bromwich. From left to right, back row: Colin Wilkey, Stephen English, Stephen Bishop, Douglas Smith, Paul Aldus, Middle row: Martyn Smyth, Stephen Tippins, Andrew Panetta, Clive Ogilvy Smith, Adrian Stanley. Front row: Martin Screech, Tony Spokes. All except Paul moved on to Lockleaze Secondary School.

Romney Avenue Junior School football team, 1968–1969 season, who played eighteen games, winning eleven, drawing two and losing five. They scored sixty-two goals, conceding twenty-four. From left to right, back row: Reg Perry, Colin Wilkey, Wayne Tidcombe, David Miles, Colin Pitt, Colin Smyth, Mr Michael Day. Middle row: Bobby Screech, Derek Jones, Stephen Bishop, Philip Church, Stephen English. Front row: Kevin or Gary Wheeler, Gordon Cox. Mr Day taught at the school from 1968 to 1981, as deputy-headmaster from 1971.

Romney Avenue Junior School chess club, 1972. From left to right, back row: Julian Maxwell, Mr Geoffrey Green, Susanne Bowden, Robert Hawkins. Front row: Mark Hoskins, Russell Smyth, Ian Coleman, Adrian Harvey, David Clatworthy.

Romney Avenue Juniors fourth year netball team, 1966-67. From left to right, back row: Linda Elvins, Heather Cox, Yvonne Bishop, Miss Hughes. Front row: Janet Clark, Eileen ?, Colleen O'Brien, Teresa Purkis, Wendy Jackson.

Mothers and young family members watch the junior school sports day, in the summer of 1956. Looking at the camera are Winifred 'Winnie' Hurley, seated fifth from the left, on her left are Edna Gadsby and Ethel Freestone; great friends who all lived in Brangwyn Grove. Presumably it's a Monday as the washing is out in the rear gardens of the houses in Brangwyn Grove.

Competitors in the junior school sports competitions, in 1956, seem to have adopted fancy dress for the races. Maurice Freestone is the boy on the left of the picture, in what appears to be his mother's dress. Romney Avenue Infants' School is the building in the distance.

The subject of the classroom display is medieval castles in this Romney Avenue Junior School picture of 1972. Putting the pictures on the wall are members of Miss Goodchild's class three, from left to right: John McBride, Peter Hawkins, Wayne Lewis, Russell Smyth.

The three girls pictured during a sewing lesson, c.1960, are left to right: Anne Peacock, -?-, Gillian ?. Anne Peacock lived in Brangwyn Grove and her father, John, used to sell toffee apples from the back of his van.

Above: Romney Avenue Juniors, 1964. From left to right, back row: Steven Jeremiah, Michael Viner, Jeffrey Lewis, Andrew Aldum, Tony Marshall, Michael Grenfell, Keith Ferguson, Leslie Lloyd, Timothy Pike, Gregory Malpas. Third row: Hilary Hendy, Susan Slade, Ruth Lawrence, Alexandra Winslett, Lorraine Coles, Elizabeth Burnham, Jane Vickerman, Carol Bridges, Jill Murray, Linda Bridges. Second row: Hilary Jones, Janice Gasson, Sarah Beech, Jacqueline Townsend, Mrs D.E. Fahy, Pauline Wheeler, Jean England, Jane Pavey, Margaret Hook. Front row: Ian Sloggett, Peter Jones, Colin Dibbins, Alan Dibbins, Geoffrey Dunn.

Opposite above: Romney Avenue Juniors, 1952-1953. From left to right, back row: Duncan Campbell, Alan Siddle, Terry Jarrett, James Reynolds, Bobby Isaacs, -?-, Keith Elsbury, Michael Beveridge, John Phillips, John Radnedge. Third row: Roger Farr, -?-, -?-, -?-, Heather Johnson, Pauline Pimm, Christine Bye, Pat May, -?-, -?-. Second row: Margaret White, -?-, Marcia Cox, Kay Nation, Ann Sheppard, Carole Lavis, Hilary Bennett, Maureen Hampton, Judith Lovemore, Pauline Adams, Diane Perry, Josephine Williams. Front row: Joan Hitchings, Desmond Tippins, -?-, -?-, Judeth Worgan, Terry Hill, Pauline Atkins, Bobby Hale, Valerie Dowling.

Opposite below: Romney Avenue Juniors, 1952-1953. From left to right, back row: -?-, George Hunt, Keith Elsbury, -?-, Clive Bennett, -?-, Michael Beveridge, John Phillips, Roger Dainton, -?-. Middle row: Raymond Edmonds, -?-, Hazel Horsham, Maureen Belcher, Pat White, Cynthia Row, -?-, Ann Wilkins, Angela Herbert, -?-, -?-, Mr Tanner. Front row: Diane Williams, -?-, -?-, -?-, Joan Hitchings, Diane Atkins, Pamela Sloggett, Carol Smart, Valerie Dowling, Pat Sadler, Sandra Lavis. The teacher, Mr Bob Tanner, or as he was affectionately known, Mr 1s 6d! The word 'Bob' was a colloquial term for 1s and 'tanner' slang for 6d, hence Mr 1s 6d.

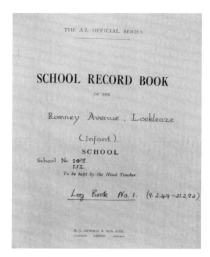

The cover of Romney Avenue School log book. The junior school opened on 7 February 1949, taking possession of just four rooms, three for children and one for general purposes, as the school building work was incomplete. Eighty-five children attended on that first day with forty of them staying for dinner. Miss D.S. Lloyd the school's first headmistress was supported on the opening day by staff, Miss E. Harris, Miss M.T. Lewis and Miss E.E. Morris, and the school secretary Mrs M. Martell. A second group of children were admitted on 1 March, twenty-two from Upper Horfield and nineteen from Ashley Down. An additional intake of fifty-three pupils was admitted on 21 March from Filton Avenue School.

The minister of education, the Rt Hon. George Tomlinson, officially opened the school on 9 March 1949. Alderman Charles Richard. Gill, the Lord Mayor of Bristol and F.C. Williams, chairman of the Education Committee were amongst the dignitaries attending the ceremony. The same minister officially opened the infants' school on Friday 13 April 1951 at a ceremony held at Southmead Secondary School.

Romney Avenue second year infants, 1961-62. From left to right, back row: Miss D.S. Lloyd (headmistress), Adrian Rogers, Andre Kirby, David Peters, Keith Smith, Lee Bailey, Christopher McGrane, Christopher Knapp, Barry Riley, Miss Celia H.M. Bovey (teacher). Third row: Diane Stone, Andrew Price, Wendy Annette, Reggie Smart, Linda Jones, Robert Richardson, Kathleen Wollacott, Tommy Harper. Second row: Michael White, Marina Diamond, John Osborne, Catherine Jones, Clive Beake, Elizabeth Taylor, Brian Wadman, Julie Naish. Front row: Susan Broom, Valerie Cooper, Ruth Nelmes. Miss Dorothy Sarah Lloyd (1910-2004) the schools first head undertook her teacher training at St Matthias College, Fishponds. It was originally called the Gloucester and Bristol Diocesan Training Institution for School Mistresses.

Romney Avenue first year infants, 1960-61. From left to right, back row: Mark Leonard, Lee Bailey, Stephen Barker, John Osborne, Martin English, Miss Sheila C. Connett. Third row: Elizabeth Jay, Julie Naish, Julia Stone, Linda Jones, Valerie Cooper, Diane Stone, Jane Gaydon. Second row: Susan Broom, Elizabeth Taylor, Elizabeth Paul, Leslie Tanner, Wendy Annette. Front row: Dennis Elmore, Michael White, Graham Smith, Brian Wadman.

Romney Avenue Infants, c.1966. From left to right, back row: -?-, David Maxwell, Teresa Long, Terry Stone, Gina Hill, Raymond Devonshire, Angela Cooper. Third row: Timothy Clack, Deborah Vickerman, -?-, Julie Sumner, Mark Priddy, Angela Nash, Wayne Tidcombe, Jayne Winter. Second row: -?-, -?-, -?-, Geoffrey Hook, -?-, Nigel Withers, -?-. Front row: Gary Wheeler, -?-, David Miles, -?-, Paul Kirby.

Plenty of outdoor activities to occupy these infant school children in the summer sunshine, 1960s. Adjoining each classroom was an open-air teaching space in the form of a wide terrace. As well as the paved playing area, there was a play garden that contained sandpits, a pool and a 'Wendy house'.

The Romney Avenue chess club of 1963 met during school lunch breaks to play challenge matches against fellow members. They also played in the Bristol Schools chess league. From left to right, standing: –?–, –?–, Peter Jones. Sitting on far side of table: Ian Sloggett, Michael Grenfell, Timothy Pike, –?–. Near side of table: Gregory Malpas, Geoffrey Dunn, Leslie Lloyd, Tony Marshall.

Romney Avenue Infants, *c.*1955. From left to right, back row: -?-, Robert Lott, Lydia Thorn, -?-, ? Williams, Paul Searle. Middle row: Elizabeth Wintle, -?-, Sylvia Wadman, Margaret Corbin, Miss ?, -?-, Bernice Hawker, Susan Cockram, -?-. Front row: -?-, Geoffrey ?, Andrew Malpas, David Clarke (?), Craig Horton.

Romney Avenue Juniors second rugby XV 1958–59. From left to right, back row: Mr Hammacott (headmaster), -?-, -?-, Philip Hedges, -?-, Ian Isles, Mr Shore. Third row: Michael Watson, David Llewellyn, -?-, Geoffrey Darby, -?-, -?-. Second row: Barry Watts?, 'Nobby' Clarke, David Coombes, Derek Slater (?), Ian Newman. Front row: -?-, -?-.

Romney Avenue Infants, November 1961. From left to right, back row: -?-, Douglas Smith, Susan Vizard, Stephen Brown, Teresa Purkis, Alan Graves, Julie Thomas, Miss D.S. Lloyd (headmistress). Third row: Barry Lane, Susan Walsie, Stephen Fermandell, Ann Bray, Martin White, Yvonne Bishop, Peter Wintle. Second row: Danny Long, Robert Hook, Jeffrey Rogers, Christine Davis, Andrew Panetta, Jill Hedges, Mark Garrett, Susan Searle, Andrew Richardson. Front row: David Jacobs, Mary Fowler, Andrew Priddy, Christine Connelly.

A pause during their lesson, for these infant school pupils, to pose for this classroom photograph to be taken, c.1958. From left to right: Andrew Malpas, Mary Wollacott, Anne Pike, Paul Searle, Gillian Skuse.

8

AROUND LOCKLEAZE

An aerial view, taken in the 1960s, showing part of Horfield, to the left of the railway line, and the south-western corner of Lockleaze, to the right. Downman Road, Morris Road and the block of flats, named Danby House, were part of phase II of the development of the Lockleaze estate. By 1966 the new residents had moved into these properties. Dovercourt Road is the road running parallel to the west of the railway line, with Constable Road Bridge beyond the two gasometers. Construction of the Horfield housing estate commenced in 1925.

This picture of escaped cows was taken from the front bedroom of No. 4 Haydon Gardens, c.1962, indicating that there was still a working farm in the vicinity. To the immediate left of the telegraph pole is Keith Elsbury's pre-war MG TC parked outside No. 14, which Keith lovingly restored and drove for many years. The telegraph pole has only one line running from it as few people had a phone in those days; the public telephone box on Romney Avenue was heavily used.

Purdown Farm, centre of picture, is adjacent to the partially built Haydon Gardens, the square with a tree in the middle of the green. Orpen Gardens adjoins. The farm was located in a field known as Purdown or Stanley Furlong according to the 1839 Stapleton Tithe Map. The low level buildings on top of Purdown are the (mostly wooden) huts used to service the anti-aircraft gun site. After the war they were taken over by squatters and demolished in the 1960s. Romney Avenue Junior and Infants Schools have not been built yet in this 1947 photograph.

Cotman Walk residents celebrate the coronation of Queen Elizabeth II with a street party. The Queen was crowned at Westminster Abbey on 2 June 1953 and children at this party were presented with a free commemorative mug. David Richardson, his brother Michael, Nigel Bly, Mr Jacobs, Olive East, Ellen East, Mrs East, Margaret Clark and her sister, Mrs Clark, Olga Sims, Mrs Jean Marsh and Anita Marsh have been identified in this picture.

Another group of Lockleaze residents celebrate the Queen's coronation in the summer of 1953. This street party took place in Landseer Avenue and featured such entertainment as running races for mums and dads whilst carrying raised open umbrellas. The 'banquet' appears to be nearing its conclusion as glass desert bowls are evident on the trestle tables, as well as an empty milk bottle. Individuals gathered around the table include: Mrs Milsom, her son John, Mrs Watts, Mr and Mrs Adams, Mrs Godfrey, Mrs Harding, Mr and Mrs Shore.

A group of Landseer Avenue children take time out from the street party to pose for the camera, with Mrs Beatrice Burgess, the proprietor of the post office in Gainsborough Square. The youngsters are the prize winners in the fancy-dress competition, judged by Mrs Burgess, which was held before the tea party commenced. From left to right: Wendy Harding, Denise Shore, Hazel Jarrett, John Radnedge, ? Radnedge, Clive White. Lindra Shore stands behind the 'policeman'.

The fancy-dress competition now over, the children sit down for their afternoon Coronation tea. All the youngsters were given a party bag containing mementos of the big day that parents had collected from various sources. Reginald Harding is the man standing at the far end. The girls immediately in front of him include: Wendy Harding, Lindra Shore, with her arm raised, Maureen Phillips, Pauline Adams and Barbara Exley. Mrs Phillips and Mrs Godfrey are standing next to Lindra Shore with Mrs Donachie, back to the camera, and Mrs Watts in the left-hand corner. Mrs Warfield in the headscarf stands behind her daughter Kathleen, with Mrs Jarrett snr next to her. Others include: Raymond Phillips, Ian Shore, Keith Jarrett and Roger Donachie.

The Church of St Mary Magdalene with St Francis was one of the many churches built in new housing estates on the outskirts of the city. It consisted of an octagon for the body of the church overlapping an elongated hexagon for the chancel and lady chapel. Prefabricated reinforced-concrete units designed for industrial buildings were used throughout. Decoration was provided solely by the materials themselves (except for some stain on the woodwork), the concrete being in varying shades of grey, by the selection of aggregates, to emphasise the various functions of the parts. The building included an engraved glass window by J. Hutton, a particularly fine chapel window in concrete and thick glass by Margaret Trahearne, depicting the Fifteen Mysteries, a font cover by Gerald Scott, and a figure in concrete of Christ by Ernest Pascoe. This was the second church to serve the people of Lockleaze. The original Church of St Francis stood in Dovercourt Road, Horfield and was replaced by this building built to the designs of T.H.B. Burrough in 1956, and with its startling outline was a prominent feature of Gainsborough Square. Unfortunately the church developed 'concrete cancer' and the cost of restoration proved prohibitively expensive for the congregation. The building became structurally unsafe and was closed, being demolished in 1996. The parish tried to save its works of art, but unfortunately when attempts were made to remove the statue of Christ it crumbled into powder. Only the window by Hutton was saved. The church site is now occupied by housing, and Gainsborough Square is much the poorer for the loss of such a prominent structure.

Lockleaze Community Centre, Cameron Walk taken in the 1970s. The wooden structure, built by voluntary labour in the 1950s, was at the heart of community activities throughout its existence until its demolition in the 1980s, when the Community Association moved to the former St James' Church hall. Marion Hawker recalls learning rock 'n' roll there on Tuesday and Friday evenings in the late fifties/early sixties. The spire of St Mary's Church is visible above the rooftop with the Pastime Centre, Brangwyn Grove, in the distance.

The Revd Terry Barr, back to camera, conducts a Remembrance Day service at St Mary's, Gainsborough Square, Sunday 11 November 1984. Kevin Brennan, Sandra Trueman, Mike Trueman, Sarah Brennan and Gordon Stevens are amongst those gathered opposite the minister, with George Petherall to his left. Members of the Royal British Legion are also in attendance. The Blue Boy public house, left, and the police station are the two prominent buildings on the far side of the square.

Michael Richardson stands in the rear garden of his house, No. 57 Cotman Walk, in the early 1960s. Behind, looking towards Constable Road, is undeveloped land extending to the railway line, used as a play area by local children and as allotments. Blake Road and Linnell Close were built on the parcel of land at the end of the decade.

Young members of the Stone family in the rear garden of their house, No. 8 Herkomer Close, in 1970. From left to right: Philip, Diane holding baby David, and Terry. Like many properties in Lockleaze, part of the garden is being utilized to provide fresh vegetables for the family. St Mary's Church, built in 1956, can be seen across Gainsborough Square in the distance.

Valerie Nash, in uniform, and Carol Bridges stand outside Val's house, No. 70 Brangwyn Grove, in 1971. Julie Nash can be seen in the back seat of her mother's Morris mini car. Valerie joined the WRAC (Women's Royal Army Corps) in April 1971, five months after leaving Lockleaze School, and is pictured whilst on leave.

The 50th (Shaftsbury Crusade) Company Boys' Brigade Band march along Cameron Walk towards Gainsborough Square, sometime in the 1980s. There was a close association between the local Boys' Brigade Company and the secondary school. The two buildings are the police station (left) and the Lockleaze Club for elderly residents, now the Cameron Centre, home to the local community organisation Lockleaze Neighbourhood Trust.

Known to local residents as 'the Dungeons', the remains of Pur Down
gun emplacement, looking north, as it appeared around 1962.

An extract from an article by Nicholas Roberts:

During the Second World War Bristol, with two aircraft factories, important docks, railways and factories, had many targets listed by Nazi Germany's Luftwaffe, but it was not until the eve of the Battle of Britain that any permanent anti-aircraft sites were built. By 20 July 1940 there were five fixed sites out of a total of eight, one of which was located on Pur Down ridge. Each site was equipped with four heavy, large-calibre anti-aircraft guns.

The Heavy Anti-Aircraft (HAA) units were manned by the Royal Artillery, often in conjunction with the Territorial Army. The main heavy anti-aircraft gun to be used was the Vickers 3.7in, a weapon large enough to be effective up to 40,000ft, but easily assembled or taken down in a few minutes. It came complete with large straddle legs, which supported it in action, and an advanced array of electronic gear. Each gun carried batteries and dials of instruments, illuminated at night, to enable the gun-layer to adjust the elevation and degree of the barrel according to the directions given by the 'predictor'. The latter was an instrument which, when fed with information from the 'height finder', provided details of the enemy aircraft's speed, height and ETA, all essential for accurate aiming. The shell weighed 28lbs and could reach an altitude of some eight miles. As the complete cartridge weighed half a hundredweight, loading the 3.7in gun was no speedy operation, yet an efficient team could fire at least eight rounds per minute.

When the possibility of a long-drawn-out battle, lasting years rather than months, became a reality the permanent sites were transformed into miniature villages, a battery or half-battery often having its own mess, canteen, cookhouse, sickbay, maintenance shops, sleeping quarters etc. A half-battery, capable of maintaining a nominal roll of about 140 men, would have operated four guns (eleven per gun), with eight men on the predictor and four on the height finder, plus ancillaries such as medical staff, fire picquet and guards. As the gun site had to be operational twenty-four hours a day, seven days a week, leave was taken in rotation.

The four gun-pits of each site were centred around the command post, and linked to the magazines by a concrete track. Around the pit a reinforced-concrete or brick wall protected the gunners and gun, and a blast mound was built outside the pit. Alongside six of the façades of the octagonal pit were iron ammunition magazines, each with doors, and each containing rounds already fused. External shelters housed the gun crew and the limber gunner's maintenance recess. The site, like the battery office, operations room and command post, was constructed half underground, the excavated material used for the surrounding mounds. At the entrance to the gun pits was a pair of hinged armour-plated doors, closed during a raid, but normally left open. A similar pair was fixed at the other end of each pit. In most cases the gun pit walls were rendered with a mortar mix, and then the whole unit camouflaged in black, dark green and dark brown paint. A camouflaged net would probably have been draped over each pit during daytime, only the barrels of the guns protruding. All tracks were painted black, and the minimum amount of local vegetation was removed. Even during the day the batteries would have been nearly invisible from the air, their deadly stings being safe from attack unless seen during firing. An anti-aircraft gun fired at night emitted a 25ft-long flame from the muzzle.

The actual number of enemy aircraft destroyed during the war as a direct result of Bristol's barrage, including those that crashed whilst returning, was probably less than a dozen. The night fighters were far more successful, but the very existence of heavy guns, the cracking of bursting shells overhead and the sheer effort put into their work by their gunners supported the morale of the Bristolians.

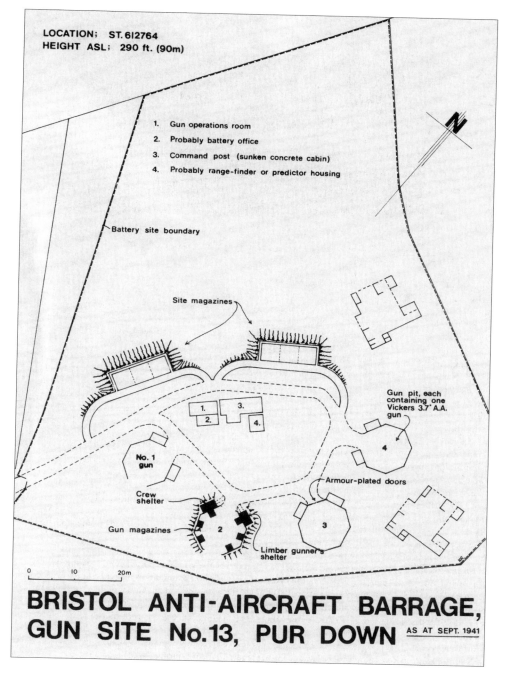

LOCATION: ST.612764
HEIGHT ASL: 290 ft. (90m)

1. Gun operations room
2. Probably battery office
3. Command post (sunken concrete cabin)
4. Probably range-finder or predictor housing

Battery site boundary

Site magazines

Gun pit, each
containing one
Vickers 3.7° A.A.
gun

4

No. 1
gun

Crew
shelter

Armour-plated doors

Gun magazines

2

3

Limber gunner's
shelter

0   10   20m

BRISTOL ANTI-AIRCRAFT BARRAGE, GUN SITE No.13, PUR DOWN
AS AT SEPT. 1941

A map of Pur Down gun emplacement as it would have appeared in September 1941. It was thought by many that there was only one gun on the site resulting in the affectionate nickname 'Purdown Percy'. One of the units stationed there during the war was 238 Battery, 76 HAA Regiment Royal Artillery.

The construction of St James' Church on Romney Avenue is underway, *c.*1952; built by the Presbyterian Church to replace the old St James' Church in the Horsefair, Bristol, which had been destroyed in 1940 during the Blitz. The congregation uniting with Trinity Presbyterian Church, Cranbrook Road, the church was opened to serve all church people in Lockleaze. The adjacent church hall, since sold to the community association to replace the community centre on Gainsborough Square that had to be demolished, was once a thriving centre for the youth of the church and for special church events.

The laying of the foundation stone of the new church by Dr Joseph Bacon, moderator of the General Assembly, 17 November 1951. The Revd Peter McCall is the minister on the left. The service for the opening and dedication of the church took place on Wednesday 29 October 1952, being attended by the then moderator of the General Assembly, the Right Revd Andrew Prentice. The first minister of St James' was the Revd Michael Drummond Whitehorn (1922-1999).

The Revd Ernest C. Marvin preaching at one of his Sunday evening services at
St James' in the 1960s. The church had a large local following under the charismatic
ministry of Revd Marvin who served at Lockleaze from 1955 to 1972. One of Revd
Martin's initiatives was to open the youth club on Sunday evenings following the
forty-five-minute church service; the only proviso being that youngsters attended the
evening service if they wanted to visit the club.

The funeral procession along Romney Avenue, in 1967, of Arthur McGill aged sixty-
four, an elder of St James' Church. The Revd Marvin is the minister walking on the
pavement at the head of the funeral cortege, with the Revd Brian Phillips, his assistant
at St James', leading the column of mourners walking in the road.

Bristol Constabulary, Sub-Divisional Police Station, Gainsborough Square. The opening ceremony was performed by the Lord Mayor of Bristol, Cllr. Kenelm Dalby on Monday 10 August 1964. The programme for the ceremony provides the following information:

Prior to 1947 the land on which the new station stands and many acres of land around it were used for agricultural purposes. Since then an extensive municipal housing estate has been developed covering an area of 220 acres and containing 1,164 dwellings and an estimated population of 4,100. The new station, with inspectors' quarters, was built by Messrs. Floyd Agar & Co. Ltd, the contract sum being £34,688, and comprises: on the ground floor – parade room, general office, report writing room, interview room, found property room, drying room, inspectors' office, sergeants' office, charge room, fingerprint office and two cells. A separate entrance is provided for the inspector's quarters; on the first floor – police women's room, staff kitchen, mess room, recreation room, CID sergeant's office, CID constables' office, and a three-bed-roomed flat for the resident Inspector. There is a large yard containing a garage for three cars, cycle accommodation and dog kennels.

Opposite above: Mr and Mrs Niblett ran the sub-post office and newsagents on Gainsborough Square for a number of years in the 1960s. This is their staff Christmas party at Lockleaze Community Centre, Gainsborough Square in 1965. From left to right, back row: Gordon Niblett, Bill ?, Ronald ?, Molly Comley, Jean Gadsby, Christine Stevens, Harriett Tucker. Front row: Christine Niblett (née Nicks), Joyce Watts, Rose Gibbs, Mrs Niblett's brother, Brenda Cooper, Evelyn Owen, Mrs Sylvia Niblett, Mr Reginald Niblett, Mrs Hurley, Mrs Edna Gadsby, Barbara 'Babs' Eveson.

The celebrations are in full swing as the party goers take to the dance floor to do the conga. 'Babs' Eveson leads the conga line, with Janet Gadsby behind her. Sylvia and Wilf Cooper are the couple facing the camera, fifth and sixth in the line, with Eileen Gibbs eighth and Joyce Watts ninth. Family and friends were also invited to the Niblett's staff party together with some of the company 'reps' who visited the shop.

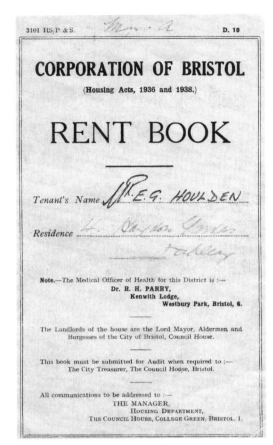

CORPORATION OF BRISTOL

(Housing Acts, 1936 and 1938.)

RENT BOOK

Tenant's Name *E.G. HOULDEN*

Residence *4. Haydon Gardens Lockleaze*

Note.—The Medical Officer of Health for this District is :—
Dr. R. H. PARRY,
Kenwith Lodge,
Westbury Park, Bristol, 6.

The Landlords of the house are the Lord Mayor, Aldermen and
Burgesses of the City of Bristol, Council House.

This book must be submitted for Audit when required to :—
The City Treasurer, The Council House, Bristol.

All communications to be addressed to :—
THE MANAGER,
HOUSING DEPARTMENT,
THE COUNCIL HOUSE, COLLEGE GREEN, BRISTOL, I.

Some of the first people to move into Lockleaze were Edward and Vera Houlden who occupied their newly built house on 17 November 1947. The illustration is the front cover of their rent book for No. 4 Haydon Gardens, the tenancy belonging to E.G. Holden. The net weekly rental was 14s 6d, with an additional 7s 6d for rates and water charges, making a total weekly payment of £1 2s 0d. Some interesting details from the first rent book are: the tenancy agreement is for 'Houses for the Working Classes' – the phrase had vanished on the next rent book in May 1952; in 1947 Eddie Houlden would have been earning little more than £2 10s per week, so £1 2s was a substantial proportion of his wage; the extra tenancy agreement inside the rear cover applied to 'houses lighted by electricity', this phrase had vanished by 1952 when the next rent book commenced. The story continued up to 19 June 1972 when the rent was £8.94 per week, when Eddie bought the house for £2,000 under Mrs Thatcher's new 'right to buy' law.

Eddie and Vera Houlden in the garden of their home at No. 4 Haydon Gardens, c.1949. They moved to Lockleaze in November 1947 and lived the rest of their lives in the house. The properties in the distance are at the top end of Romney Avenue; in due course Mulready Close, Rackham Close, Gilray Glose, and Fairacre Close will be built on the land behind the Houldens.

Eddie Houlden sits in his garden with his son Bernard on his knee, whilst neighbour Alan Mays looks through the wire-mesh fence. The double-fronted Purdown Farm, with a big cow shed on the north side of it, is the building behind. The farmhouse was demolished *c.*1955 and Fairacre Close built on the site.

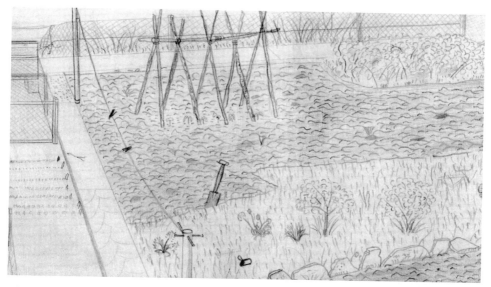

The back garden of No. 4 Haydon Gardens drawn in 1961 by Mike Houlden as part of his art homework. The view is from the rear bedroom window and shows the effort Eddie Houlden put into supplying the family with fresh vegetables and fruit. He also kept chickens in the run on the left of the drawing, which many people did, often building the coops from wood salvaged from the old anti-aircraft barracks on Purdown.

Built in 1970 the British Telecom (BT) Tower on Purdown is one of twelve reinforced concrete towers owned by BT in the United Kingdom. It is used mainly for point-to-point microwave links and forms part of the BT microwave network, and is also used for radio broadcasting in the Bristol area. The tower is 58m tall to the top gallery with the lattice structure on the gallery adding an additional 8m Taken in the summer of 1970 this picture shows the new concrete tower alongside the original metal version, later demolished. Fairacre Close, built on the site of Purdown Farm, is in the foreground.

Mike Houlden stands beside his first car, a second-hand Morris Cowley that was fitted with a replacement engine. The car cost £65, which Mike earned working during the university summer holidays at Witts' bakery in Ashley Hill. According to Mike, it was a real rust bucket, with a three-speed column-change gearbox, no seat belts, but he drove for six years and did about 50,000 miles. The picture was taken outside No. 4 Haydon Gardens in 1966.

A double-decker bus passes the junior school (on the right) on its journey up a deserted Romney Avenue to Gainsborough Square, *c*.1952. Housing development on the estate is still in progress with Mulready Close under construction on the left. The open fields and ridge of Purdown are in the distance.

A 1983 view from Bonnington Walk Bridge looking back at Constable Road Bridge. The remains of Horfield Station platforms are visible in the foreground. Opened on the 14 May 1927 as Horfield Platform, its name was shortened to Horfield in November 1933. It closed on the 23 November 1964. Danby House flats, Morris Road and Downman Road in the distance. Wordsworth Road is on the right. Lockleaze Lane once turned off left just after Constable Road Bridge.

Other local titles published by The History Press

Barton Hill Revisited

BARTON HILL HISTORY GROUP

This second collection of over 200 previously unseen photographs takes a fresh look at Barton Hill, a lively community in East Bristol. Aspects of everyday life are featured, from schools and churches to public houses and shops, including Max Williams' much-loved toy shop. The Great Western Cotton Factory, the University Settlement and the Barton Hill Swimming Baths are some of the landmarks that are remembered, and events such as the departure of the last steam trains from the Barrow Road railway yard are also recalled.

978 0 7524 3557 2

Easton, Eastville and St Jude's

VERONICA SMITH

This charming collection of over 200 images brings to life the people and places of this fascinating area of Bristol. From the corner shops that grew in abundance in the area in the early part of the twentieth century to the many community groups who gathered together here, the reader is taken on a nostalgic journey around the district. Easton, Eastville and St Jude's will delight long-time residents and newcomers alike.

978 0 7524 3712 5

Around Stapleton

VERONICA SMITH

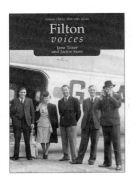

Illustrated with over 200 photographs, this pictorial history is a remarkable evocation of life in and around the Stapleton of yesteryear. From timeless vistas of the Frome Valley to snapshots of the bandstand at Eastville Park, local sporting heroes at Alexandra Park, Fishponds Lido and Coronation Day parties, this volume provides a nostalgic insight into the life and changing landscape of the area around Stapleton.

978 0 7524 3059 1

Filton Voices

JANE TOZER AND JACKIE SIMS

This book brings together the personal memories of people who lived and worked in Filton from the 1930s, vividly recalling the farms and fields before they were lost to housing. The voices tell of childhood games, the close-knit community, shops and entertainment, as well as the devastating effects of bombing raids on the aircraft factory, cheek by jowl with the village. The stories are complemented by a hundred photographs drawn from the private collections of the contributors.

978 0 7524 3097 3

If you are interested in purchasing other books published by The History Press, or in case you have difficulty finding any History Press books in your local bookshop, you can also place orders directly through our website

www.thehistorypress.co.uk